AN INTRODUCTION TO
PICTURE
FRAMING

AN INTRODUCTION TO
PICTURE
FRAMING

VIVIEN FRANK

A QUINTET BOOK

This edition published in 1995 for:
Shooting Star Press, Inc.
230 Fifth Avenue, Suite 1212
New York, NY 10001

ISBN 1-57335-300-0

Reprinted 1995

This book was designed and produced by
Quintet Publishing Limited
6 Blundell Street
London N7 9BH

Creative Director: Peter Bridgewater
Art Director: Ian Hunt
Designer: James Lawrence
Illustrator: Danny McBride
Project Editors: Judith Simons and
Henrietta Wilkinson
Editor: Betty Floyd
Photographer: Ian Howes

Typeset in Great Britain by
Central Southern Typesetters, Eastbourne
Manufactured in Hong Kong by
Regent Publishing Services Limited
Printed in Singapore by
Star Standard Industries (Pte) Ltd

CONTENTS

INTRODUCTION

There are many different ways to frame a picture. This book shows you how to achieve decorative, stylish and pleasing effects without spending a vast amount of money at a framer's shop.

Certain pictures, for example old masters and other valuable works, are best left to the professional framer, and some decorative techniques, such as gilding, are so specialized that they are outside the scope of this book. But there are still numerous picture framing techniques that an interested and creative person can easily undertake.

A frame plays a major role in the total visual impact of the artwork it surrounds – it can enhance or distort. For this reason you should take great care in selecting materials. The choice of materials is subjective; in general, it is governed more by taste than by rules. If possible, look around friends' homes, art galleries and museums for styles, ideas and current fashions.

The frame isolates the picture from its surroundings and gives it importance. But it should also act as a bridge relating the work to those surroundings and to its general environment. It is important, therefore, to create a balance; this has a great deal to do with achieving the right proportions – a skill that will come with experience.

The techniques used throughout the book are easily mastered, and the equipment and materials required need not be expensive. You can, for example, give a child's painting importance by framing it with a mount created to complement it; you can make a decorative frame using fabric to match the decor of a room; or you can enhance a special photograph in a simple wooden cut-out frame. This book is designed to dispel some of the mystique surrounding the interesting craft of frame-making and to encourage readers to enjoy creating a variety of frames. A little patience and preparation is all you need to design and create professional-looking picture frames.

TOOLS AND EQUIPMENT

PAPER AND CARD MOUNTS

1 (from left to right) Smooth-surface hardboard, standard hardboard, acid-free backing card, grey backing card.

2 Assorted papers including watercolour paper and textured paper.

3 Standard mountboards, including acid-free, conservation quality and black core.

4 Mountboards with textured surfaces, for example, Ingres, linen, flecked and fabric.

3

4

TRADITIONAL MOULDINGS

■ A selection of traditional style mouldings, with gold and natural wood finishes predominating.

MODERN MOULDINGS

A selection of modern style mouldings. The mouldings themselves are quite plain in comparison with traditional styles, but are available in a wide range of colours and finishes.

TOOLS

1 mitre box
2 tenon saw
3 mitre clamp
4 frame clamp
5 try square
6 hand plane
7 drill bits
8 glass cutter
9 nail set/nail punch
10 pin hammer
11 pliers
12 small screwdriver
13 bradawl
14 multi-screwdriver

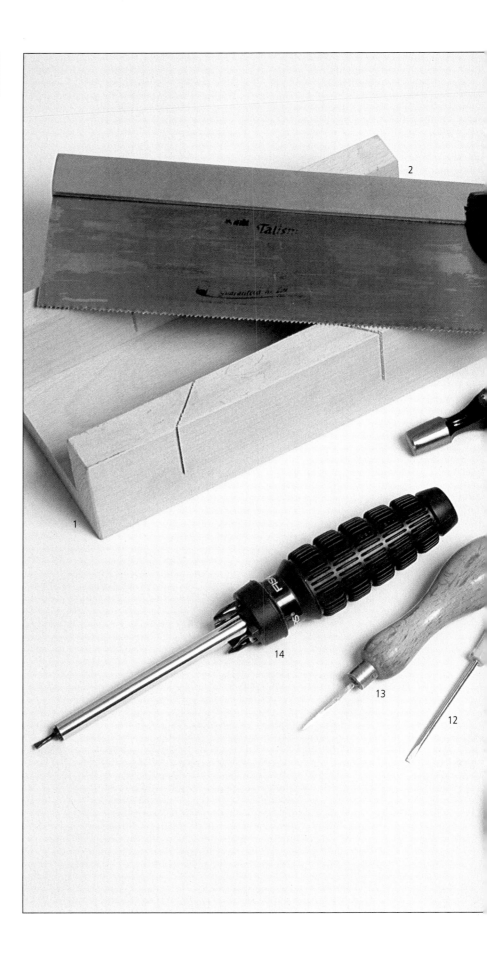

EQUIPMENT

1 double-side adhesive tape
2 gummed tape
3 self-adhesive tape
4 plastic ruler
5 mount cutter with integral ruler
6 corner gauge
7 mount cutter
8 scissors
9 circle cutter
10 paint
11 pencil
12 paint brushes
13 chinagraph pencil
14 assorted felt-tip pens
15 compasses
16 craft knife
17 metal set square
18 glue pen
19 cutting mat

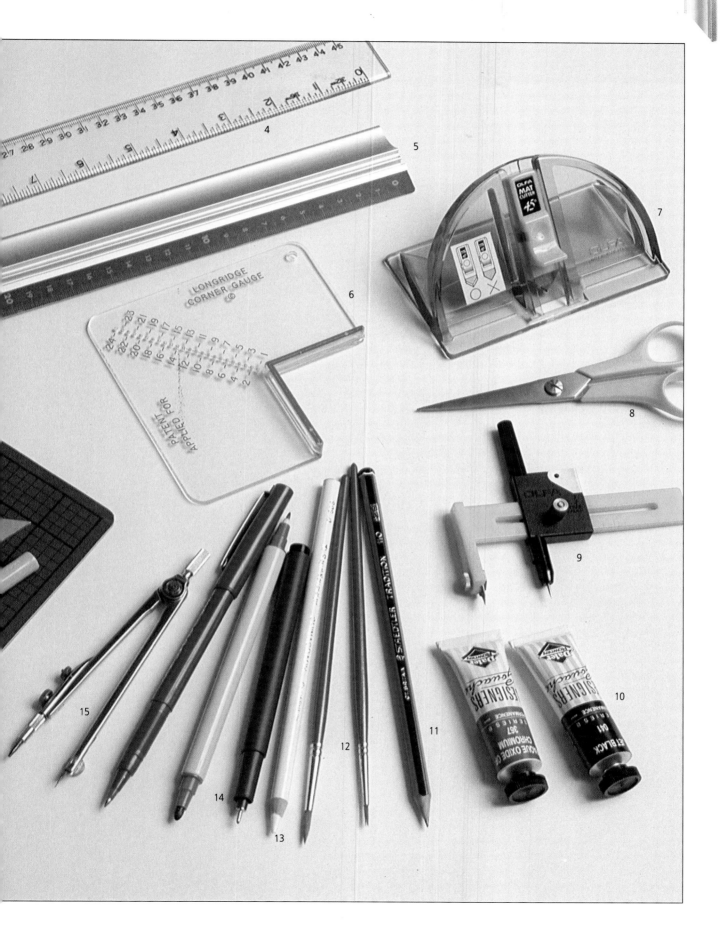

4

5

6

7

8

9

10

11

12

13

14

15

ACCESSORIES

1 plastic self-adhesive
  hangers
2 veneer pins
3 brass picture wire
4 strut hinges
5 clips for 'frameless'
  frames
6 various sizes of
  screw eyes
7 D-rings
8 screw rings
9 triangle hangers
10 rings and clips
11 rivets for D-rings
12 glaziers' points
13 turn clips
14 mirror clips
15 metal centre
   hangers
16 frame stand
17 plastic-coated
   picture wire
18 gummed hangers

LIGHTWEIGHT FRAMES

CARDS WITH SLITS

This is a simple way to frame a picture or photograph. If done with care, it can produce a surprisingly effective look.

EQUIPMENT

■ pencil
■ ruler
■ craft knife or scalpel
■ paper or lightweight card

VARIATION 1

To enhance the picture, choose card for the frame in a colour that complements it. Take extra care in deciding on the width of the surround as this will also affect the final look. For a small picture about the size of a postcard, you can incorporate a strut in the frame to make it free-standing (see page 48).

2 If using a strut to make this frame free-standing, follow Fig. 1 on page 48. After scoring, fix in position.

3 Carefully insert the corners of the picture into the slits in the frame.

VARIATION 2

Another simple card frame with slits is shown in Fig. 2. Here the slits are less evident; they also provide more support for a larger picture.

TIP

Both these 'frames' could be decorated using one of the methods explained later in this chapter or in the section dealing with mount decoration in the next chapter.

1 Again, take care in selecting the colour of the card for the frame.

2 Using the diagram in Fig. 2, prepare and cut two slits in each corner.

3 A gummed hook fixed to the centre back of the card is used to display the completed frame – this is suitable for lightweight frames only.

4 Insert each corner of the picture in one slit and out of the other. The two slits provide a band across each corner to hold the picture firmly.

1 Decide on the overall size of the frame, mark the dimensions on a piece of card and cut out. Draw faint lines to show the position of the picture and then mark the corners symmetrically, as shown in Fig. 1, to show where the slits will be. Cut the slits.

SIMPLE CUT-OUT FRAME

This is a more decorative but equally straightforward way to frame a small picture.

E Q U I P M E N T

- as previous project
- acetate (optional)
- elastic bands
- thin dowel
- hole punch

P R E P A R A T I O N

Cut out two pieces of card to the required dimensions for the frame. Decide on the width of the surround and cut a window in one piece. Attach the picture to the other piece and place the piece with the window cut-out on top. Acetate can be placed over the 'frame'.

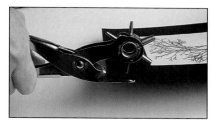

1 Punch two holes at the top and two at the bottom (see Fig. 3).

2 Cut two pieces of dowel the width of the card. Thread an elastic band through the two top holes and around the ends of one dowel. Repeat through the other two holes and around the ends of the other dowel – this secures the frame.

3 This frame can be displayed in a variety of ways – free-standing, with gummed hangers or with a strut.

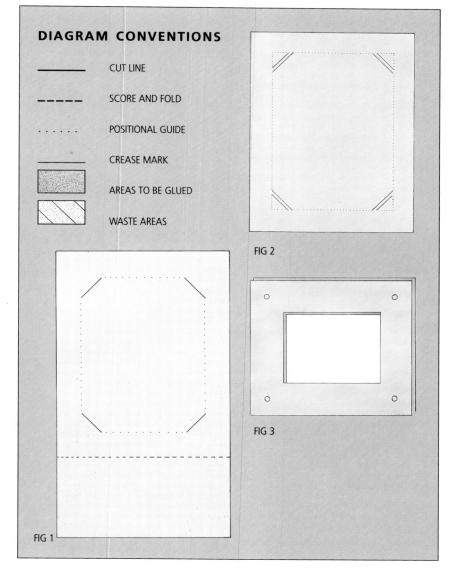

DIAGRAM CONVENTIONS

———	CUT LINE
– – –	SCORE AND FOLD
· · · · ·	POSITIONAL GUIDE
———	CREASE MARK
▨	AREAS TO BE GLUED
▨	WASTE AREAS

FIG 2

FIG 3

FIG 1

FOLDED CARD FRAMES

VARIATION 1

This technique is often used to frame photographs which are to be posted. The frame is made from a single fold of card.

As with all frames, choose your materials carefully. If the finished frame is to be sent in the post, consider the size of readily available envelopes when planning the project.

EQUIPMENT

- pencil
- ruler
- craft knife or scalpel
- paper or lightweight card

1 Cut the card to the required size and lightly mark the centre. Lay the ruler along this line and score with the back of the knife or a bone folder, taking care not to cut through the card.

2 Fold the card along the crease mark and secure the picture in position using either the slits method shown on the previous page or with invisible photo-mounts or photo-corners.

3 The frame protects the photograph in the mail and can also be used as a stand.

VARIATION 2

A simple folded card frame can be embellished to make a more decorative frame. Examples are shown on the following pages. This frame has an extra fold so the photograph is completely enclosed.

EQUIPMENT

- as previous project
- piece white paper
- scissors
- photo-mounts

PREPARATION

▌ The basic method can be adapted. Decide on the overall dimensions of the frame. This frame was designed to fit a standard envelope – its dimensions, when folded, are 0.5cm (¼in) smaller in both length and width than the envelope.

▌ The piece of card from which the frame was made was 15.5cm × 33cm (6in × 12¾in) – that is, the same length as the folded card and three times the width. Score the card so that it is divided into three equal parts.

1 In this frame, the photograph is displayed through an oval opening. To make the oval, start with a piece of thin, white paper the same size as one of the three sections of the frame and fold it into quarters. Decide on the height and width of the opening and mark half of each of these measurements on the piece of paper (see Fig. 1).

2 Draw a curve to join the two marks (see Fig. 2). Then cut along the line and unfold the paper – an oval has been created (see Fig. 3). If the shape is not pleasing, try again.

3 Position the oval cutout in the required position on the middle third of the piece of card (see Fig. 4). Draw around the oval.

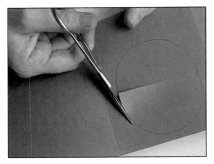

4 Carefully cut the oval out.

5 Place the photograph in position on the reverse side of the righthand third of the card and stick in place with photo-mounts, so that the photograph shows through the window. Then stick this to the centre section.

6 The lefthand third of the card can be folded either to the front to cover and protect the photograph in the envelope or to the back to display.

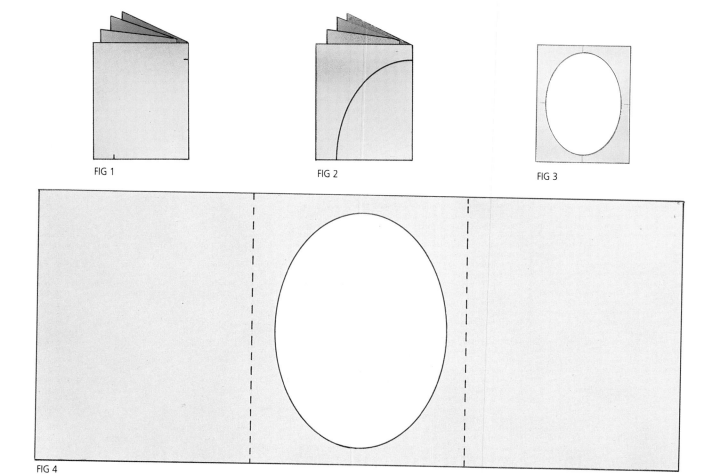

FIG 1

FIG 2

FIG 3

FIG 4

DECORATED FOLDED FRAMES

VARIATION 1

The photograph in this example was framed with a single fold of card. To prevent this delightful picture from being overwhelmed by the strong colour of the frame, the card was decorated with sponged-on ink, using shades from the photograph, to soften the colour and enhance the picture.

1 Cut a window in one layer of the card and carefully sponge the ink around the border, taking care not to colour the backing area by protecting it with a sheet of waste paper.

2 Glue the photograph to the uncut area of the card, and then glue the window section on top.

VARIATION 2

A child's drawing was framed in the same manner as the photograph in the previous project, but the size and proportions of this frame are different. There is a wide border, and it is decorated with a stencilled design which complements the picture.

EQUIPMENT

- pencil
- ruler
- craft knife or scalpel
- paper or lightweight card
- stencil material (oil-coated paper, template plastic or acetate)
- stencil brush or sponge
- paint, crayons or felt-tip pens

1 Draw the shapes on the stencil paper and cut out. Try using template plastic or acetate for the stencils so you can see where the design is being positioned.

2 When the stencil is ready, position the cutout shape on the frame and, using paint, crayons or felt-tip pens, apply the colour.

3 To hang the completed frame, attach a gummed hook to the back of the card – this type of hook is suitable for lightweight frames only.

ORIGAMI PICTURE FRAME

For this project you will need lightweight paper; you can choose a colour that complements your photograph or postcard. If you are planning to frame a standard-sized postcard measuring 14.5cm × 10.5cm (5¾in × 4¼in) with a vertical (or portrait) picture, you will need a piece of paper 29cm × 39cm (11½in × 15½in).

It is easy to adapt the measurements to suit different sizes of pictures. The first measurement should be double the height of the picture and gives the height of the frame. The second measurement will depend on how much, if any, of the paper at the side of the picture you want to show. However, the width of the frame should be at least 2½ times the width of the picture. The picture opening will always be square; it is not necessary to show the whole picture as the width can be adjusted by pushing in the sides. To check whether your measurements are suitable, experiment with a piece of scrap paper.

EQUIPMENT

- pencil
- ruler
- lightweight paper

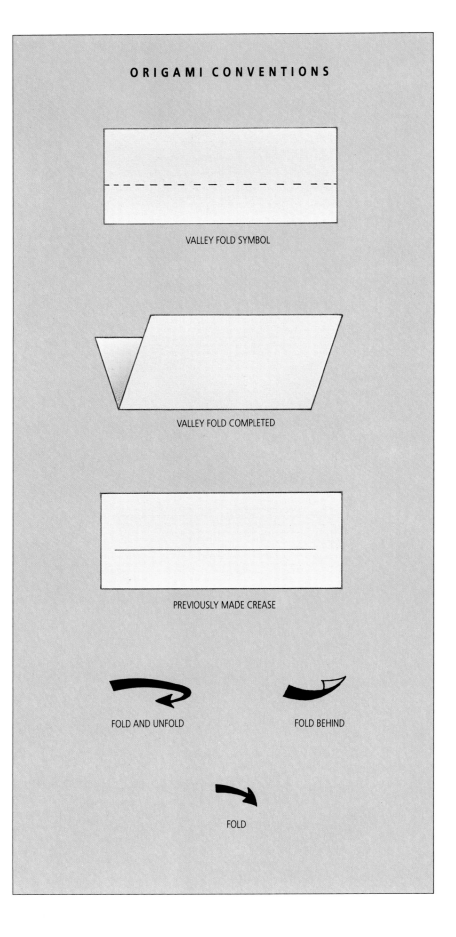

ORIGAMI CONVENTIONS

VALLEY FOLD SYMBOL

VALLEY FOLD COMPLETED

PREVIOUSLY MADE CREASE

FOLD AND UNFOLD

FOLD BEHIND

FOLD

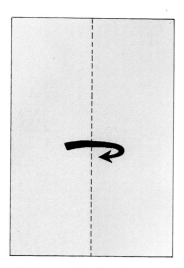

1 Fold the paper in half and then unfold.

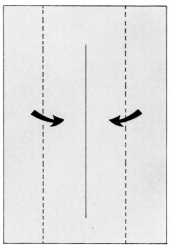

2 Fold the two outer edges to the creased centre line.

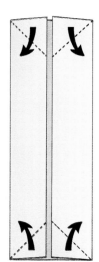

3 Fold the four corners from the centre to the outer edge; make sure to fold only the top, single layer of paper.

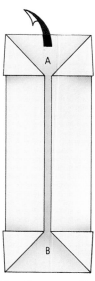

4 Now, holding the paper with the folds towards you, gently curl the paper away from you so that you tuck the side marked A into the side marked B.

5 The frame is now complete and the picture can be carefully tucked into the diamond shaped space. For a triangular effect, crease the centre back, insert the picture and then crease the two sides. If the postcard to be framed is very stiff, it can be inserted into one side between steps 3 and 4.

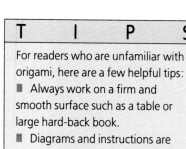

T I P S

For readers who are unfamiliar with origami, here are a few helpful tips:
- Always work on a firm and smooth surface such as a table or large hard-back book.
- Diagrams and instructions are equally important; often one helps to clarify the other. Looking ahead to the next diagram will show how the model should look after the instruction has been carried out.
- Make the folds slowly and accurately so that the creases are sharp.

FOLDED CORNERS AND BACKING

Another way to display a postcard, photograph or small drawing is to create corners in which to slip the picture. This method is an easy way to make a more decorative presentation than the slit methods explained on page 18.

EQUIPMENT

- lightweight card
- paper
- scrap card
- pencil and ruler
- scissors
- craft knife
- glue

PREPARATION

▌ To begin, you will need a piece of lightweight card cut to the same size as the picture. This can be coloured, but most of it will be hidden by the picture.

▌ You will also need to cut a piece of paper, the same size as the picture, to be used as a backing. This can be in a colour that complements the picture.

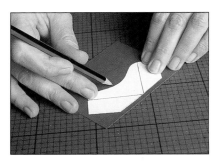

1 Using a piece of scrap card, cut a template of one of the shapes in Fig. 1. Now, using the template, cut four shapes from the paper. If the picture is very large or very small, you may have to alter the size of the corner pieces proportionately.

2 On these pieces, score along the dashed lines shown in the diagram.

3 Fold these glue flaps back and position around the piece of card. Glue in place.

4 Now glue the matching piece of paper over the whole of the back so that the glue flaps are covered. It is possible to make a strut as explained on page 48, or to use a frame stand as shown in the accessories section on page 16.

5 Insert the picture; the frame is finished.

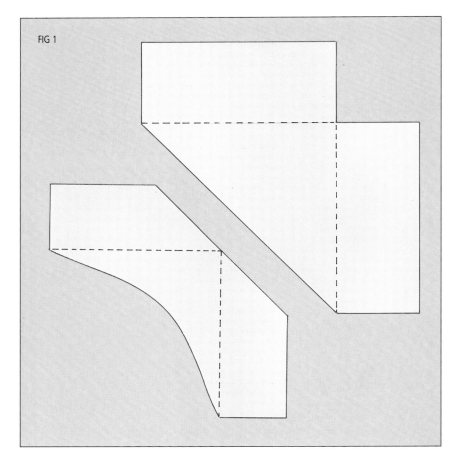

FIG 1

MOUNTBOARD FRAMES

SOME THOUGHTS ON MOUNTING

◼ This selection of undecorated mounts shows the vast range of colour and texture available to the frame maker.

The use of a mount, even without a frame around it, can and should greatly enhance a piece of artwork. The colour and the dimensions of the mount and the material used to make it should all be selected with great care.

A mount should be more than a rim of colour surrounding the work. The colour should complement the work and link it with the frame, when a frame is used. It should also harmonize with the environment in which the finished piece will be displayed.

The width of the mount governs the amount of 'space' around the work. This 'space' distances the work from its surroundings – for example, 'busy' wallpaper. A wide mount also tends to emphasize the work; a narrow one can crowd it.

A mount also protects the work by preventing it from coming into contact with the glass. This contact could cause damage from condensation over a period of time. To further protect the artwork, you should use acid-free materials for the mount even though they may seem expensive. If the piece of work to be framed is valuable, you may want to consider using conservation quality materials. Until recently mount card was made from untreated wood pulp with high proportions of acid and other impurities which, over a period of time, migrated from the mount into the artwork and caused damage and discolouration. Acid-free mount card is made from rag pulp; conservation mount card is made from chemically treated wood pulp. You can also use acid-free backing paper so that the

work is sandwiched between acid-free materials and acid-free glue and hinges to fix it to the backing material (see page 40). In this way the work is protected as much as possible.

A mount can detract from the art if it is not wisely selected. The mount should complete the piece, not compete with or overwhelm it. Take time over the choice of colour and size. Hold corner samples of various colours against the work to check the possibilities. Remember also that mountboard is available with different textured surfaces and if a ready-made one is not quite right, you can make your own (see pages 34 and 36). You can also reduce the severity of a mount, if necessary, in several ways, some more simple than others. These include:

◼ added depth (see page 38)
◼ double window (see page 40)
◼ double mount (see pages 40–41)
◼ v-cuts (see page 42)
◼ wash-lines (page 44)
◼ marbled paper lines (page 46)

T I P S

Many optical illusions occur with mounts:

◼ They can make the artwork look smaller so it is important to work out the appropriate width for each piece of artwork.

◼ Conversely, a mount can give a small picture greater importance.

◼ A dark picture surrounded by a light-coloured mount will seem smaller than the reverse.

◼ The visual centre of a picture is always above the geometric centre – especially in a 'bold' piece of art. If the work is divided exactly in half, the finished appearance will seem top-heavy. To offset this effect, many pictures have a mount that is deeper at the bottom than at the sides and top.

PICTURE COLLAGE

An inexpensive and effective way to display a large number of photographs or sketches is to mount them on a large piece of mountboard, and then hang it or pin it to a pinboard. The mountboard can be in a colour that makes the pictures stand out if that is the effect you want. This method is an interesting way to display pictures that are not important enough to be framed individually. It might be used as a design source for an artist, for example. The pictures can be fixed to the mountboard either with glue or with photo-mounts.

STRAIGHT-CUT MOUNTS

The black and white drawing shown in this project was designed on the computer and was so striking that it required a simple, even stark treatment such as this black mountboard with a black core so that the eye is not drawn to the cut edge. Mounts are traditionally cut with a bevelled or sloping edge. This leads the eye into the picture, creates an illusion of depth (this can be accentuated by the choice of materials) and prevents shadows from being cast on the work. In this case a straight cut was used so that the shadow it cast would emphasize the perspective of the picture.

It is important to be accurate at all times so the finished work appears professional – inaccuracies show and can cause complications when making the frame.

E Q U I P M E N T

- selected mountboard
- ruler
- pencil
- metal ruler
- set square
- craft knife
- cutting mat or waste card
- masking, brown paper or fabric tape
- double-sided adhesive tape

P R E P A R A T I O N

▌ Start by measuring the area of the artwork that will be visible – in this example 29cm × 18.5cm (11⅜in × 7¼in). This is called the 'sight' area. These measurements allow for the mount to cover the edges of the picture by 0.25cm (⅛in).

▌ Now decide on the dimensions of

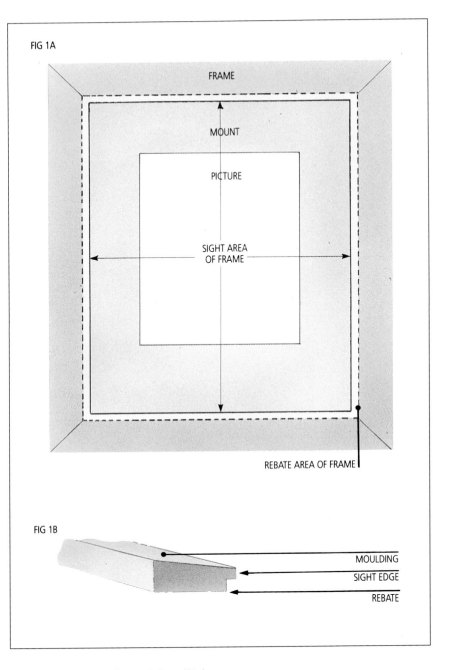

FIG 1A

FRAME

MOUNT

PICTURE

SIGHT AREA
OF FRAME

REBATE AREA OF FRAME

FIG 1B

MOULDING

SIGHT EDGE

REBATE

the mount: sides and top, 7.5cm (3in); bottom, 9cm (3½in). With these two sets of measurements, you can calculate the overall size of the mount: 44cm × 35cm (17⅜in × 13¾in). If the artwork is to be framed eventually the size of the rebate of the moulding will have some bearing on the overall dimensions of the mount as the rebate will cover some of it (see Fig. 1a and 1b).

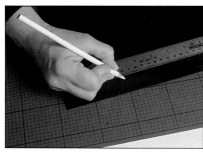

1 Mark the outer edges of the mount carefully on the mountboard and check to make sure everything is square – right angles at all corners. In this instance a white chinagraph pencil was used so the lines would be clearly visible on the black surface.

3 Now mark the window on the reverse side of the mountboard. Measure from the outer edges and check to make sure that the corners are square.

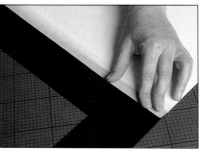

5 Now the mount, backing board and picture are ready for assembly. Lay the mount and the backing face down with the top edges touching. Stick them together with masking tape, brown paper tape or fabric tape. This is called hinge mounting.

2 Lay the board on the cutting mat or on waste card. Using a very sharp blade and a metal ruler, cut out the mount and a piece of backing card the same size.

4 The window is now ready to be cut out. Place the mount on the cutting mat or waste card, lay the ruler along the pencil line and, holding the knife at a 90° angle, cut along the line. Hold the ruler very firmly so that it does not move – if necessary clamp it in place.

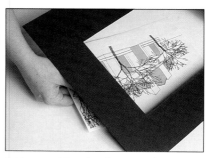

6 Next, position the picture on the backing board and flip the mount over. By lifting the mount slightly it is possible to move the picture around until you get it into the right position. Then fix the picture to the backing board with double-sided adhesive tape.

T   I   P   S

■ If the cuts meet in the corners, the window will drop out. If it does not, cut carefully into the corners.

■ A razor blade or emery board can be used to neaten a slightly ragged edge.

■ Keep the piece you cut from the mount for use on a smaller picture or for practice.

■ To fix a valuable piece of artwork to the back board (see step 6), use acid-free paste to attach two small strips of torn acid-free paper to the edge of the picture. Then stick the top of the strips to the backing board with gummed tape.

BEVEL-CUT MOUNTS

For this drawing a single mount with a bevelled edge was used (to draw the eye to the drawing). The colour was selected to give a 'quiet' effect.

EQUIPMENT

- selected mountboard
- ruler
- pencil
- metal ruler
- set square
- craft knife
- waste card
- mount cutter

PREPARATION

■ Decide on the 'sight' area – this is the amount of the drawing that will be visible through the mount window – 32cm × 26.5cm (12½in × 10½in) in this case. Now decide on the width of the mount – sides and top 7cm (2¾in) and bottom 8.5cm (3¼in). With these two sets of measurements, you can calculate the overall size – 47.5cm × 40.5cm (18½in × 16in). Mark this carefully on the sheet of mountboard and check the measurements to make sure everything is square.

■ Lay the board on the waste card. Using a very sharp blade, cut out the board and a piece of backing card the same size.

■ Now mark the window on the reverse side. Measure from the outer edges, and check to see that the corners are square.

1 Position the ruler or straight edge according to the type of mount cutter you use. Make sure the blade is sharp and that it is set to the correct depth for the mountboard. If the blade is too deep, the cutter will be hard to move and if it is not deep enough, it will not cut through the mountboard and the window will not drop out.

2 Pay particular attention to the corners – try not to over-cut them as this will show on the right side – they should look like this.

TIPS

■ It is essential to practise on some spare board to get the feel of the cutter.

■ Do not use a cutting mat with a mount cutter, as bevel-angled cuts do not 'self-heal'.

■ When cutting the mount, turn it clockwise so you can see the beginning of the previous cut as you approach it and know where to stop.

3 If the corners are cut short, carefully slip the craft knife or a razor blade into the cut, complete the corner and lift out the window.

4 Assemble the mount, backing board and picture as explained in the previous project on page 30.

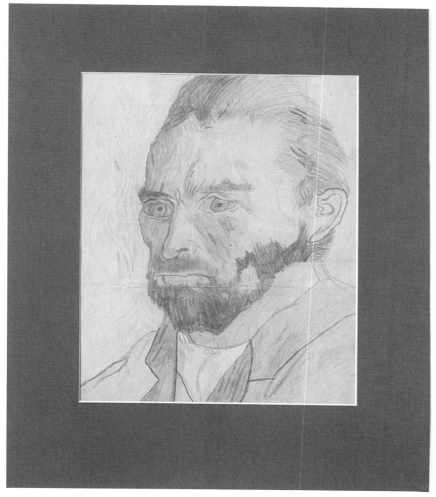

COVERING MOUNTS: WITH PAPER

In some cases, you may decide that a plain mount would be too severe for the picture you want to frame. One way to deal with this problem is to cover a mount of the appropriate size with some form of decorative paper. Alternatively, the mountboard itself could be decorated, using either of the techniques already described (see pages 22 and 23).

In this example, a shade of blue echoing the delicate blue threads of the Japanese paper contained in the etching was selected for the mountboard. This element was further emphasized by covering the mountboard with a semi-transparent Japanese paper with a 'lacy' finish which allowed the blue to show through.

EQUIPMENT

- selected mountboard
- ruler
- pencil
- metal ruler
- set square
- craft knife
- waste card
- mount cutter
- covering paper
- adhesive suitable for paper
- scrap paper
- roller (optional)

PREPARATION

Cut the mount to size as explained in the previous two projects and cut out the window. It is not essential to cut a bevelled edge, but the overall effect will probably be better if you do.

1 Spread glue thinly and evenly over the whole mount – too much glue will soak through the covering paper and not enough will leave an uneven appearance.

2 Position a piece of Japanese paper, cut to the size of the mount plus 2cm (¾in) all round, on the mountboard and cover with scrap paper. Apply pressure evenly over the four sides and leave to dry under a pile of books.

3 Turn the mountboard so the Japanese paper is face down, on a clean work surface. Cut diagonally across the outer corners of the paper so that they will be mitred when turned over.

4 Apply glue to the edge of the mountboard and turn over the edges of the Japanese paper neatly.

5 Cut a window in the centre of the paper, leaving a margin of 1.5cm (½in) on all sides. Cut very carefully into the corners so that it is possible to turn over the edges. Apply glue and turn neatly.

6 Finish as described in the previous two projects.

TIPS

- If you plan to frame the mounted picture, step 3 could be omitted and the paper trimmed to the same size as the mount.
- It is, of course, possible to follow this project using any light- to medium-weight paper. It would be wise to check the reaction of the paper to the glue before starting.

The black and white photograph shown here is mounted in a striking but simple way. A straight-cut black mount is covered with a medium-weight good quality cartridge paper. The outer edges were 'deckled' as described below.

E Q U I P M E N T

- selected mountboard
- ruler
- pencil
- metal ruler
- set square
- craft knife
- cartridge paper
- mount cutter
- fine brush or medicine dropper
- adhesive suitable for paper

2 Then, very gently, pull the edge away from the main area, to create a deckled edge.

3 Glue the paper to the mount and finish as already described.

1 Using a fine brush or medicine dropper, 'draw' a line of water and allow it to soak in for a short time.

4 The finished mount has a dark edge.

COVERING MOUNTS: WITH FABRIC

This mount is particularly suitable for fabric pictures such as embroidery, tapestry and patchwork because it has a soft look. There is a great feeling of space already contained in the small embroidery chosen for this project and in order to emphasize this, a large and light-coloured mount has been used.

EQUIPMENT

- selected mountboard
- pencil
- metal ruler
- set square
- craft knife
- waste card
- mount cutter
- covering fabric
- adhesive suitable for fabric

- scrap paper
- roller (optional)
- iron (optional)

PREPARATION

First, cut the mount to size as explained in earlier projects in this section. Use white or cream mountboard to make sure the colour does not show through the material.

Next cut out the window; it is not essential to cut the mount with a bevelled edge, but the overall effect is probably better with a bevel.

Cut a piece of material that is 1.5cm (½in) larger all round than the mountboard. Try to choose a material that does not fray easily.

1 Apply PVA adhesive to the mountboard in a thin layer and leave to dry. Then position the material on the board, cover with scrap paper and carefully iron over the area – the heat will reactivate the glue. Check that the fabric has no wrinkles and is stuck down all over. Allow to cool under a weight.

2 Turn the mountboard so that the material is face down on a clean surface. Cut diagonally across the outer corners of the material so that they will be mitred when turned in. Apply glue to the edge of the mountboard and turn the edges over neatly.

3 Cut a window in the centre of the material leaving a margin of 1.5cm (½in) on all sides. Cut very carefully into the corner so that you can turn the edges over. Finish as described previously.

TIPS

- Special care should be taken when using velvet to avoid flattening the pile. It may be best to avoid the iron technique for glueing; and if framing the mounted print, insert a spacer between the mount and the glass under the moulding rebate (see Fig. 1).

- If using ordinary adhesive, disregard step 1 and proceed as follows. Spread glue thinly and evenly over the whole mount – take care as any excess glue will soak through the fabric. Position the material on the mountboard and cover with scrap paper. Apply pressure evenly over all four sides and leave to dry.

- If you want a more padded effect, place a thin foam sheet between the covering fabric and the mount. Foam can also be used to give a padded effect to an embroidered picture before mounting; it has the added advantage of absorbing knots and giving a smooth appearance.

4 If the mount is to form part of a conventional frame, omit the previous step and trim the fabric to the same size as the mount.

5 The softness of the fabric-covered mount enhances the work.

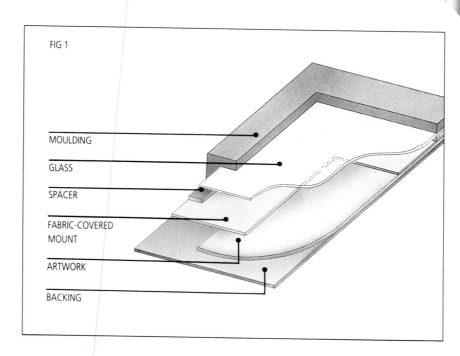

FIG 1

MOULDING

GLASS

SPACER

FABRIC-COVERED MOUNT

ARTWORK

BACKING

HOW TO MAKE A PERFECT OVAL

If you prefer, you can cut an oval window in a mount and cover the area around it with fabric to hide any slight inaccuracies. To draw an oval geometrically use the following method:

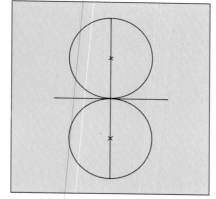

2 With a pair of compasses, draw a circle above and below the horizontal (width) line. The radius of each circle will be one-quarter of the vertical (height) line.

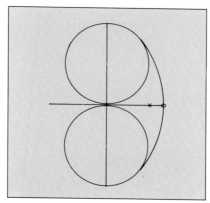

4 With this radius, position the pencil point on one end of the width line, place the compass point on this line and draw an arc joining the two circles on one side.

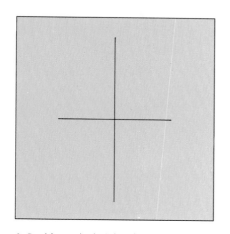

1 Decide on the height of the oval. The width of the oval will be two-thirds of this measurement. Draw these dimensions, in the form of a cross, on the mountboard.

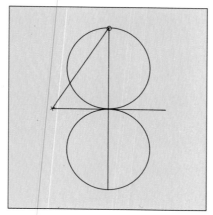

3 Take the compasses and position the point at one end of the width line and extend until the pencil point touches the top of the height line.

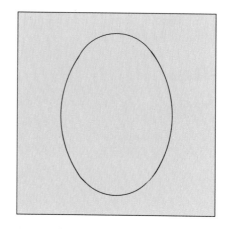

5 Move the pencil point to the other end of the width line and repeat step 4 to complete the oval.

MOUNTS WITH EXTRA DEPTH

On some occasions the artwork to be mounted is not completely flat. Although this problem can be solved by making double or triple mounts (see page 40) or a box frame (see chapter commencing on page 105), there is another way. Using a material formed by sandwiching polystyrene foam between two lightweight boards, a mount can be cut in the usual way. This material is available in several thicknesses and is extremely lightweight and versatile. It can be covered with paper or fabric as described in the two previous projects; it can also be used to create a space between mounts or between mount and artwork (see Figs. 1a and 1b).

EQUIPMENT

■ foam core board
■ metal ruler
■ pencil
■ set square
■ craft knife
■ waste card
■ mount cutter
■ lightweight covering paper
■ glue suitable for paper
■ scrap paper

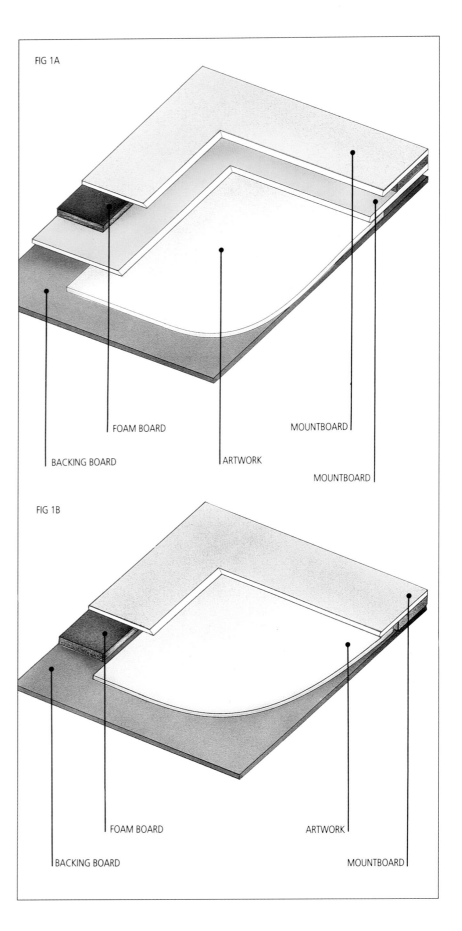

FIG 1A

FOAM BOARD

MOUNTBOARD

BACKING BOARD

ARTWORK

MOUNTBOARD

FIG 1B

FOAM BOARD

ARTWORK

BACKING BOARD

MOUNTBOARD

1 Cut the mount to the required size and prepare as in the project on page 34.

4 Before gluing, score the paper along the edge of the window so that it turns more easily.

▪ Another simple way to embellish a foam core mount is to make a second mount from a contrasting or toning piece of paper and to place this between the mount and the artwork. A dark 'lining' paper will enclose the piece.

2 Tissue paper is a delicate covering material and two layers should be used for extra strength. To ensure an adequate coverage, glue an extra piece of paper into the window corners.

3 Take particular care when turning in the paper for the window – practise first on a piece of waste to ascertain how far into the corner you should cut.

5 The finished mount has a three-dimensional look.

DOUBLE-WINDOW MOUNTS

It is sometimes necessary to cut two windows in one mount as for the bond shown here. Other instances where this might be necessary are: topographical or sporting prints which have a title under the print area; a photograph which requires a title that is not part of the design; or a set of small pictures. Take extra care choosing a colour when mounting a set of pictures, as the colours in each print may not be identical. The following method has also been used for the multiple mount on page 100.

EQUIPMENT

- selected mountboard
- metal ruler
- pencil
- tracing paper
- set square
- craft knife
- waste card
- mount cutter
- acid-free paper
- acid-free paste
- adhesive tape

1 The main problem in cutting this style of mount is the accuracy demanded. Plan this project on a piece of tracing paper first with all the measurements written in. It may be helpful to cut a dummy mount from a piece of paper to check the look and dimensions.

2 When you are satisfied with the plan, transfer the measurements to the back of the mountboard and cut out the windows.

3 This is a valuable piece so it has been fixed to the backing card with acid-free strips of paper and acid-free paste. Tear two strips of paper and paste them to the top edge of the picture.

4 These are then stuck to the backing board with adhesive tape.

5 The strip between the two windows separates the two sections of the bond and adds emphasis to both.

DOUBLE MOUNTS

This type of mount adds interest to a picture and, if it is to be framed, can also create a deeper than normal space between artwork and glass.

The mount closest to the picture is usually a darker colour than the outer one. The visible part of the inner mount should be about 0.75–1cm (¼–½in) wide. If you are using a triple mount, make the visible parts of the inner two mounts different widths to avoid a staircase effect. For a purely visual effect, you can use narrow strips of coloured paper attached to the reverse of the mount with double-sided adhesive tape (see below).

EQUIPMENT

- selected mountboards
- pencil
- metal ruler
- set square
- craft knife
- waste card
- mount cutter
- double-sided adhesive tape

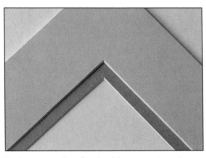

■ An example of a double mount; note that the darker coloured material has been used for the inner mount.

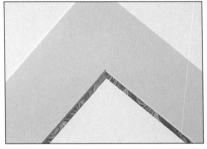

■ Plain or patterned paper can be cut into strips and applied to the back of the mount to create a simple visual effect.

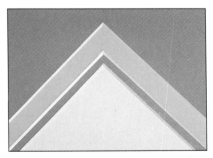

■ An example of a triple mount. Note the different widths of the two inner mounts.

PREPARATION

■ To cut a double mount accurately, follow this procedure. First decide on size of the window in the inner mount and then decide on the outer dimensions of the finished mount. The dimensions here, for example, are 16.5cm × 11.5cm (6½in × 4½in) for the window and 25cm × 20cm (10in × 8in) for the mount.

■ First cut the outer mount to size. Then cut the window 0.5cm (¼in) [this width is variable] larger all round than the inner window will be – 17.5cm × 12.5cm (7in × 5in). Do not

remove the window cut-out.

■ Place strips of double-sided adhesive tape on the back of the mountboard, positioned centrally on all four sides of the window border. Stick another strip of tape in the centre of the window cut-out which will act as a base for cutting the second window in the inner mount.

1 Cut the inner mount 24cm × 19cm (9½in × 7½in) and place it centrally on the prepared window mount. Mark the window on this, measuring from the edges of the outer mount to ensure accuracy.

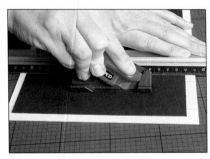

2 Working from the back, as usual, cut the second window.

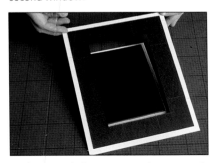

3 The two windows can now be removed.

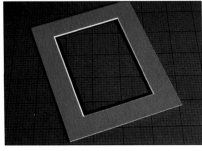

4 Turn over and the double mount is complete.

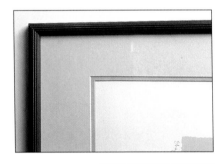

■ The subtle appeal of a double mount can be seen here. The shades of the mounts and the colour of the frame were all chosen to complement the delicate blues and greys of the screenprint.

V-CUT AND DOUBLE-BEVEL MOUNTS

Another way to add a creative touch to a picture is to use V-cuts in the mount. There are several variations within this style – a mountboard with a coloured core (as used here) can give a particularly stylish effect, or the V-cut could be made wider and used with an inner mount to create a double mount (see Fig. 1a). The same techniques used for the basic V-cut are used to create these additional effects.

EQUIPMENT

- selected mountboard
- pencil
- metal ruler
- set square
- craft knife
- waste card
- mount cutter
- double-sided adhesive tape
- masking tape

PREPARATION

■ As always, decide on the size of the window first and mark this on the back of the mountboard. It may be necessary to make this mount a little larger than usual so that the finished piece has enough 'space' to allow for the 'break' caused by the V-cut. If unsure, leave the mount excessively large and cut it down after you have completed the bevels.

■ Decide how far away the V-cut will be from the window edge and mark this second line on the back of the mountboard. Mark the V-cut line on the right side as well, either very faintly or with a short line near the edge of the mount.

1 First cut the outer window but tape it in place, with masking tape, all around without removing it. Then cut the inner 'window' and tape it in place temporarily.

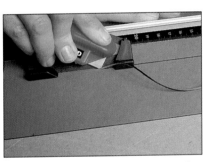

2 Turn the whole mount to the right side and very carefully cut another bevel along the marked line – the mount cutter should be on the window side of the mount.

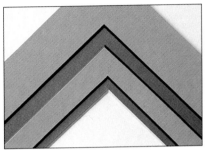

■ Alternatively, cut one mount as usual and then cut a second one with a larger window. From this piece, cut another window larger still and cut a bevel on the right side of this. Place double-sided adhesive tape on both pieces of the outer mount and place carefully in position, applying pressure (see Fig. 1b).

3 The buff coloured mount and the black core revealed in the V-cut harmonize perfectly with the delicately shaded life drawing.

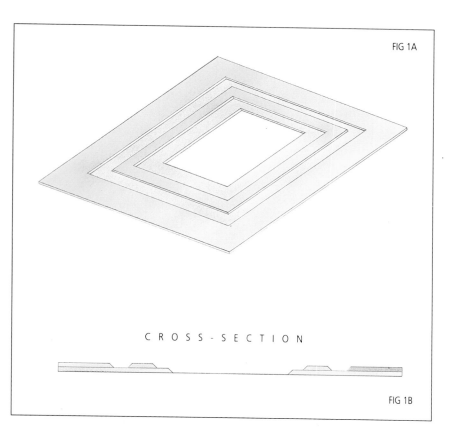

FIG 1A

CROSS-SECTION

FIG 1B

T I P S

There are many different ways of applying this type of mount-cutting:

▌ Angles or curves can be cut which will attract attention to areas of the picture (see Fig. 2).

▌ Designs can be cut into the mountboard which would allow a contrasting colour, positioned underneath, to show through (see Fig. 3).

▌ A window effect can be created by cutting the mount from three different colours which relate to the picture (see Fig. 4.).

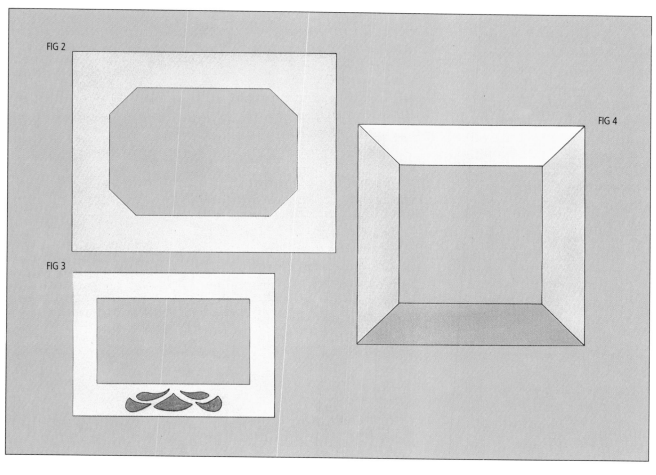

FIG 2

FIG 3

FIG 4

MOUNTS WITH WASH LINES

Lines and washes are traditionally used to decorate the mounts of watercolours and prints. They can, however, be used to embellish many other types of picture. It is important that the work be well done because bad workmanship will show. Practise on off-cuts to gain experience and to try out different combinations and spacings. It is also a good idea to test the mountboard and materials you plan to use to check their compatibility – some inks or felt-tip pens may 'bleed' on some mountboards. Lines can also be used without washes – a good way to unite several small prints or photographs mounted together.

The spacing of the lines is important. If they are too far from the window, the eye will not be held; the first line should be no more than 0.5cm (¼in) from the window. A standard and effective pattern of lines and washes is: two lines close together near the window, then a wide space for the washline, and finally two or three more lines positioned quite close together. When using the ruling pen, it is a good idea to vary the width of the line by adjusting the space between the points. The widest line will 'lead' the eye into the picture and should therefore not be next to the window as the outer lines may seem to disappear.

EQUIPMENT

- selected mountboard
- metal ruler
- pencil
- plastic ruler
- set square
- craft knife
- waste card
- mount cutter
- ruling pen
- watercolours
- mixing palette and brushes
- corner marking gauge
- sable (or good quality) brush

TIPS

- If you do not have a corner gauge, try making your own or use a ruler to mark out the line sequence on the mount.
- When selecting the colours for lines and wash, look carefully at the picture and try to choose colours that will tone with it.
- When drawing lines, take care not to make the line so wide that the ruling pen runs out of ink – it is impossible to stop and reload the pen without the break showing in the finished piece.
- Your selected wash colour should be mixed to a very pale shade and to a thin consistency. If using coloured inks, dilute greatly so that the colours do not look too bold – test the colour on waste card first.
- When applying a wash, start at one corner and work quickly, so that the first part is still damp when the wash is applied to the last side of the mount. Apply the wash in several thin layers to build up the colour if necessary. Have a few cotton buds nearby, as they can be very useful for mopping up excess wash or runs.
- If there are any small imperfections, they can sometimes be removed with a small sharp blade. Or another line might possibly cover the error. It is always worth trying a repair before starting to remake a mount.

1 Take the selected mount and cut the window as usual. Then, using a corner gauge, decide on the sequence (spacing) of the lines and mark them in each corner with a pin or a hard pencil.

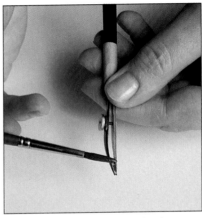

2 Load the ruling pen with ink using a brush and wiping it gently against the nib. If dipping the pen directly into the ink, wipe the edges before use.

3 Using a plastic ruler turned upside down to avoid smudging the ink or watercolour – the bevelled edge of the ruler will create a space between it and the mount – draw all the lines carefully, working from the inside line outwards and with the outer edge of the mount closest to the body.

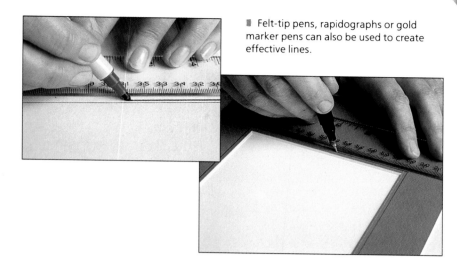

■ Felt-tip pens, rapidographs or gold marker pens can also be used to create effective lines.

4 Using a brush dipped in clean water, dampen the area between the lines so that the colour wash flows evenly onto the mount without leaving any 'tide' marks. Then apply the wash using a brush which is close in width to the required washline.

5 The colours chosen for the lines and wash in the example shown here enhance the rural quality of the watercolour painting. By using a brownish green for the lines and a paler version for the wash, the whole effect on the cream-coloured mount is an extension of the painting.

MOUNTS WITH PAPER STRIPS

Another way of adding decoration to a mount is to use narrow strips of paper or tape. Self-adhesive gold or coloured tape, available from specialist shops, can be used in conjunction with lines and washes or on its own. It is also possible to apply this tape to the bevel itself, but this is very tricky. Alternatively, a slim plastic slip fillet, made in several colours, can be placed on either edge of the mount to get this effect.

The spacing of the lines and/or strips is most important. If they start too far from the window, the eye will not be held. Therefore, the first line should be no more than 0.5cm (¼in) from the window. A standard and effective pattern for lines and strips is: two lines close together near the window, then a wider space for a paper or tape strip, and finally more lines positioned quite close together. When using the ruling pen, it is a good idea to vary the width of the lines by adjusting the space between the points.

EQUIPMENT

- selected mountboard
- pencil
- metal ruler
- set square
- craft knife
- waste card
- mount cutter
- marbled paper and/or coloured tape
- adhesive suitable for paper and/or double-sided adhesive tape

PREPARATION

▌ Take the selected mount and cut the window as usual. Decide on the sequence (spacing) of the lines and/or tapes and, using a corner gauge, mark them in each corner with either a pin or a hard pencil.

▌ Mark with a pencil the line that will have the strip – this will act as a guide. Rule the rest of the lines using the chosen medium – ruling pen, felt-tip, marker pen or rapidograph.

1 If undertaking much mount decoration of this kind, there is a tool available which can be set to cut several equal strips at a time – a multi-cutter.

2 Cut the strips of paper using a metal ruler to guide the cutter. Take great care in cutting the strips as any inaccuracies will show.

3 Lay the paper or tape strips carefully along the pencil lines. They should overlap at the corners.

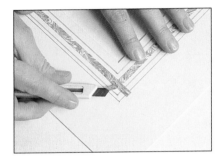

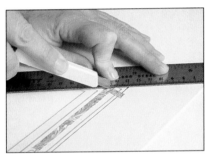

4 Using the craft knife, cut through both strips from the window outwards at an angle of 45°. Pull away the excess to leave a cleanly mitred corner. Cover the mount with a clean piece of paper and apply even pressure to the window area to ensure that the strips are completely adhered.

TIP

If self-adhesive paper and tape strips are not available, you can make your own using double-sided adhesive tape on decorative paper, but the finished appearance will not be as flat.

5 The strips on the mount pick up the colours in the picture and enhance the overall effect.

■ Here are some variations to a theme: self-adhesive gold tape (right); fine lined paper strip (far right); (and below, from left to right) plastic slip fillet used on the window edge; on the outer edge of the mount; a combined effect with a double mount edged with slim gold plastic slip fillets.

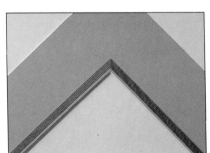

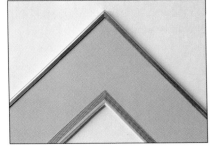

47

STRUTS

There are several ways of making struts for frames – the following diagrams show how to do this. Some are an integral part of the frame, and some are added to the finished frame. The type of strut used often depends on the weight and size of the frame.

EQUIPMENT

- lightweight card or thick card (see directions)
- pencil
- ruler
- craft knife
- glue and/or double-sided adhesive tape

CONVENTIONS TO DIAGRAMS

All dotted lines are position guides.
All dashes lines should be scored and creased.
All solid lines should be cut.
All shaded areas require adhesive.

VARIATION 1

The diagram in Fig. 1 shows a very simple support for the type of frame shown on page 18.

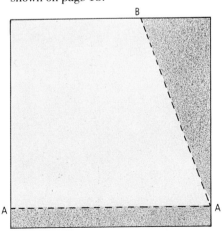

FIG 1

- Using lightweight card, cut out a piece as in Fig. 1.
- Score the lines AA and AB as in the diagram.
- Apply glue or double-sided adhesive tape to the two shaded areas.
- The base area (AA) is stuck to the centre of the stand part of the frame and the upright, triangular area (AB) is stuck to the centre of the 'frame' back.
- The angle at which the picture 'stands' can be varied by altering the angle of the line AB.

VARIATION 2

The strut shown in Figs. 2 and 3 is more a stand than a strut as it is not attached to the frame. The larger the frame, the bigger the stand should be to provide sufficient support.

- Cut out a strip of lightweight card as shown in Fig. 2 – the area for gluing is slightly narrower than the area to which it will be stuck.
- Fold into a triangular shape and glue in position as shown in Fig. 3 – make sure to leave a small gap in which to place the picture.

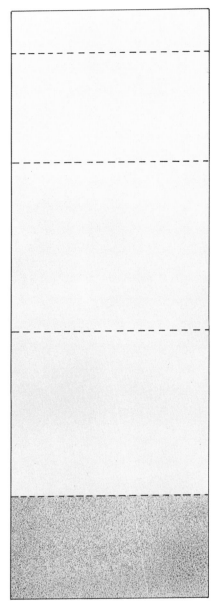

FIG 2

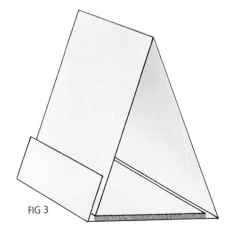

FIG 3

VARIATION 3

The method shown in Fig. 4 is probably the simplest of all, but its use is limited to a few types of frame – the project on page 26, for example.

▌ When making the back of the frame, cut an extra piece of paper or card the same size but preferably in a lighter-weight material than used for the front of the frame.

▌ Cover the back of the frame as instructed in the project and then score the strut piece and glue the shaded area directly on top of the frame back.

FIG 4

VARIATION 4

The two struts shown in Figs. 5 and 6 and Figs. 7 and 8 are similar and both are made of thicker card than the previous ones. The main difference between them is that the strut in Figs. 5 and 6 is fixed to the frame back. The strut in Figs. 7 and 8 is fixed to the support and slides under the upper tab – this is easier to make. These struts and frame backs should be made before the two halves of the frame are put together. The frames look better if the inside of the back is lined with a piece of toning paper; that way, when the picture is removed, the hole left by the support does not show from the front.

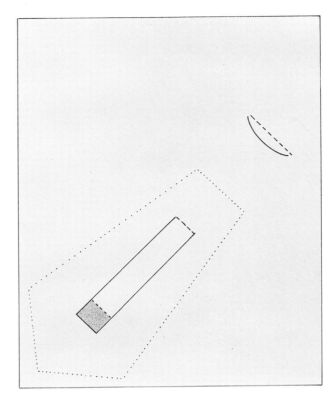

FIG 7

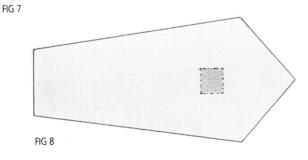

FIG 8

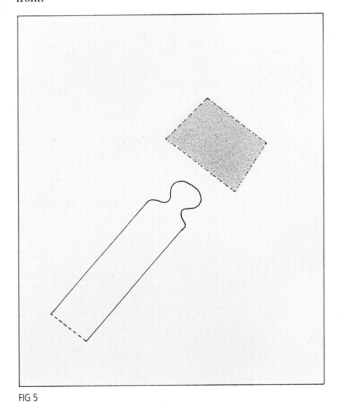

FIG 5

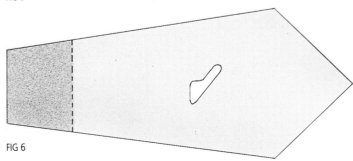

FIG 6

50

CLAY AND PAPIER-MACHE

PAPIER-MACHE MIRROR FRAME

Papier-mâché frames are fun to make for both children and adults. As they are made from paper, they are extremely light in weight but they can be made to look very ornate with a little experience. It is easy to get carried away when decorating these frames, so take care not to overpower the contents of the frame.

The two examples shown in this section are very different. The basic method – described below – has been used to frame a mirror, and the decoration is quite striking. The picture frame described in the second project on page 56 has less decoration as the shape is part of the design and the picture in the frame is powerful. The colour of the background has been chosen to tone with the picture.

Papier-mâché can be decorated in a number of ways – painting or drawing directly on to the shape, using stencils or with collage. Both of the examples in this chapter have been decorated using paint. The shape in the basic example following has only the edge painted as the centre will be covered by the mirror.

PREPARATION

▌ Cover the working area with an old cloth or newspapers and prepare the adhesive – either mix up the wallpaper paste according to the directions on the packet or dilute the PVA adhesive with three parts glue to one part water.

▌ Take the mould and cover the inside with vaseline or plastic film so that the papier mâché will be easy to remove when the layers are completed.

1 Tear up strips of newspaper and tissue, dampen the pieces and lay them neatly across the mould. Try to keep the strips as flat as possible by tearing them to fit.

2 When the mould is covered, paint the surface liberally with the paste or thinned PVA.

3 Now add the next layer. It is a good idea to use a coloured paper, such as tissue, so that layers can be seen clearly and the paper built up evenly on the mould.

4 When the mould is covered, brush on more paste or adhesive. Continue to build up the layers in this way until there are about eight layers. Put the mould in a warm place and leave it for about 24 hours to dry.

5 Carefully remove the paper from the mould and trim the edges.

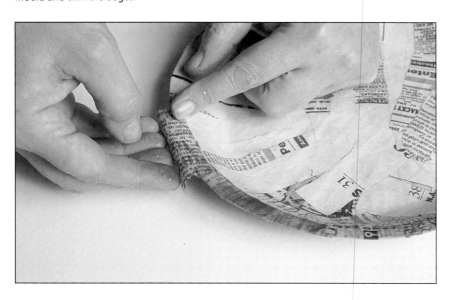

6 To get an even edge, bind the cut edge with two layers of paper. When the edges are quite dry, sand away any unevenness with a medium to fine grade sandpaper and then paint the shape on both sides with two layers of undercoat. This will ensure an even base for the final decoration.

7 Draw around the mirror and then sketch in the design on the frame with a pencil.

8 Mix the paints – gouache or poster paint – to an appropriate consistency and paint in the design.

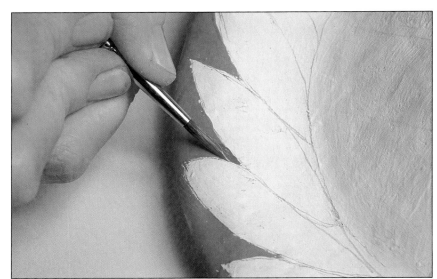

9 The black paint adds the final touch to the design as well as covering slight mistakes. The reverse side can either be painted with a single colour or decorated. For durability, give the finished frame three coats of varnish.

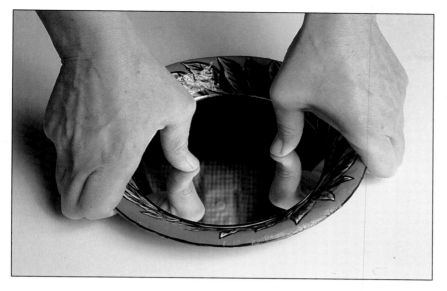

10 On the back of the mirror, put a generous amount of adhesive in the centre and 1cm (¼in) all around the edge. Then, placing the mirror in the correct position on the frame, press down firmly and hold until the adhesive has set. If the frame is slightly uneven, this pressure will take care of the problem.

11 Use the same strong adhesive to fix a hanger to the back of the mirror frame, and suspend it from a hook.

PAPIER-MACHE PICTURE FRAME

EQUIPMENT

- old newspapers
- coloured tissue paper
- wallpaper paste or thinned PVA adhesive
- pre-sealed cork floor tiles
- craft knife
- scrap card or cartridge paper for template
- masking tape
- sandpaper
- paint brushes
- emulsion paint for undercoat
- paint and varnish
- thin wooden batten
- quick-setting adhesive
- backing board
- turn clips or veneer pins

PREPARATION

First, decide on the size and shape of the frame, and then make a template from the scrap card or cartridge paper. The template can be a half or quarter of the frame if the frame is symmetrical.

TIP

If the picture is to be permanently fixed into the frame, the measurement for the backing board should be taken from the outer edges of the wooden battens. Place the picture into the frame and, using veneer pins, tack the backing board in place.

1 Draw around the template on to the tiles to form the shape of the frame.

2 Cut out the shape with a craft knife.

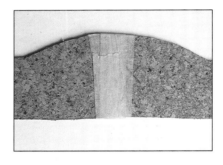

3 Unless the frame is quite small, the tiles may not be large enough. In this case the tiles were joined with masking tape wrapped around the cut shape.

4 Using the method already described on pages 52 and 53, cover the back and front of the 'frame' with layers of newspaper and tissue or coloured paper. It is not necessary to use vaseline or plastic film as the cork becomes part of the frame and there is no mould to remove. When sufficient layers have been applied, leave the frame to dry. Turn it over from time to time so that both sides dry evenly.

5 When the frame is dry, sand away any unevenness with a medium to fine grade sandpaper and then paint it on both sides with two layers of undercoat. This will ensure an even base for the final decoration.

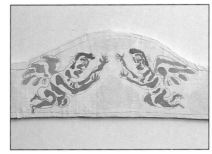

6 Sketch the design around the frame with a pencil. Mix the paints – gouache or poster paint – and paint in the design. Remember to paint the reverse side of the frame to tone with the basic colour.

7 The black paint adds definition to the shape as well as covering slight mistakes. For durability, the finished frame has been given three coats of varnish.

8 On the back of the frame, mark the size of the picture – this will give the line for the inside edge of the battens. Cut two lengths of batten for the sides and two lengths for the top and the bottom. Spread the quick setting adhesive along the battens and fix to the marked positions on the back of the frame, holding firmly.

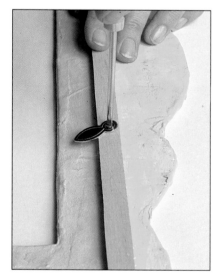

9 If the picture is to be interchangeable, the backing board should be the same size as the picture. Attach the turn clips to the battens – the number used will depend on the size of the frame. Place the picture and the backing board in the frame and lock into position by turning the clips.

10 This highly decorated papier-mâché frame would make an interesting decoration even without an insert.

■ The same template was used to make the frame shown here, but was simply painted in one colour and then varnished.

■ A simple stencilled design can produce an equally pleasing effect.

CLAY FRAME

A small decorative frame can be made using clay. A kiln is not a necessity as you can use self-hardening clay or substitute products, available from craft shops, for this project. If you use self-hardening clay, find out about the special glazes for it. Clay or clay substitutes should be used only for small frames – a maximum size of 15cm (6in) in diameter or 12.5cm (5in) square – because a larger frame could warp.

EQUIPMENT

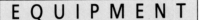

- clay of selected type
- rolling pin
- piece of polythene on which to roll out clay
- ruler
- pencil
- craft knife
- template
- 2 pieces of scrap hardboard a little larger than proposed frame size
- fine sandpaper
- card for backing
- paper adhesive for picture
- impact adhesive for finishing
- paint
- varnish
- brushes

PREPARATION

Decide on the size of the frame. A rectangular frame is easiest to make because you can use strips of clay. For a circular frame, you have to use a round template about 2cm (1in) thick.

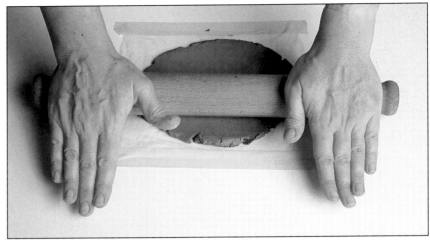

1 Working on the piece of polythene to keep the clay from sticking to the work surface, knead and flatten the clay. Then roll it out until it is about 0.5cm (¼in) thick and as long as the proposed frame.

2 Using the ruler so the edges will be completely straight, cut four strips about 2.5cm (1in) wide.

3 On one piece of scrap hardboard, draw pencil lines for guidance. Then place the strips of clay in position; the two side strips first, then the two remaining strips across the top and bottom. These strips will overlap the side strips.

4 Now mitre the corners by cutting diagonally through both strips from the inside of the frame to the outside. Remove the waste pieces.

5 Next moisten the cut edges at each corner and score with the knife point so that the surfaces are slightly rough; then press them together.

6 Smooth the top surface with the knife; if necessary, dampen slightly. This step is most important.

T I P S

The frame can be decorated in different ways:

■ It can be simply painted as in this project or additional shaped pieces of clay can be added to it. These pieces should be cut from the remains of the clay rolled out for the frame. Roll it out a little thinner and stick the shapes to the frame with moistened clay. If necessary, the design can be attached with a suitable glue.

■ Whichever method of decoration you choose, varnish the frame when it is finished.

■ Cut a piece of the backing card the same size as the frame and fix the picture in the centre of the card. The picture should be slightly larger than the window of the frame. If you wish to change the picture frequently, attach it with photo-corners.

■ To finish the frame, fix the backing card to the frame with glue or, if the picture is to be interchangeable, with narrow strips of self-adhesive Velcro on the frame and the backing.

■ To display the frame, attach a strut to the backing (see pages 48–50) to make it free-standing or fix a gummed hanger very securely to the back.

7 Place the second piece of scrap hardboard on top of the frame and carefully turn the 'sandwich' over. Lift off the hardboard and check to see that the joins are smooth on this side. Replace the hardboard, place a book on top to prevent the frame warping and/or cracking and leave to dry. When the frame is dry, gently smooth away any rough edges with sandpaper.

8 Using poster paints or gouache, paint the base colour onto the frame and allow to dry.

9 The frame can be further decorated, and varnished with a product compatible with the clay used.

CUT-OUT FRAMES

BASIC METHOD

This frame is relatively quick to make and allows for simple or elaborate decoration. As it is made from a flat piece of wood, there is no need for special equipment or for great accuracy. This type of frame is not suitable for valuable pieces of work, however, because the picture is not sealed into the frame and is vulnerable to the atmosphere.

E Q U I P M E N T

- pencil
- ruler
- craft knife or scalpel
- lightweight card
- birch plywood (0.6cm or ¼in thick)
- thin hardboard
- batten strips (0.3cm or ⅛in thick)
- hand drill
- small saw
- fretsaw
- keyhole board
- clamps
- sandpaper and wood adhesive
- paint
- brushes
- varnish

P R E P A R A T I O N

▌ As with previous projects, decide on the window and the overall size of the frame first. Draw the overall measurements on the piece of wood and cut the piece to size or have this done at the suppliers. Birch plywood is the easiest type with which to work – it cuts smoothly and can be finished to a high standard. Other types of plywood do not have these advantages.

▌ Next, prepare the wood – a little extra effort at this stage will save time later. Working in the direction of the grain (visible on the surface of the wood), gently sand the top surface. Take a damp cloth and wipe over the surface so that the area looks damp but is not saturated. Allow to dry completely. The surface will now feel slightly 'hairy' – this is called 'raising the grain' and occurs only once. If this were to happen when the frame is being painted, it would not be possible to sand the surface without spoiling the paintwork. Now sand the surface again – the wood should feel satin-smooth.

▌ Next, draw the 'window' on the piece of wood. Drill a small hole in a corner of the window area of the wood so that the blade of the fretsaw can be inserted. If the window is square or rectangular, it might be easier to make a hole in each corner to avoid having to negotiate the corners with the fretsaw. Sometimes you have to drill more than one hole because the 'throat' of the fretsaw will not reach part of the line and you have to work from two directions to cut it.

▌ Some of the more unusual pieces of equipment needed for the following projects: a keyhole board, fretsaw and G-clamps.

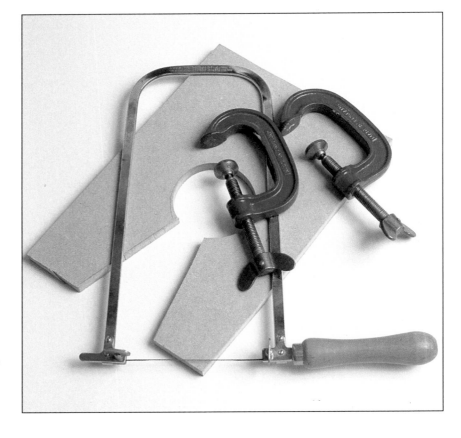

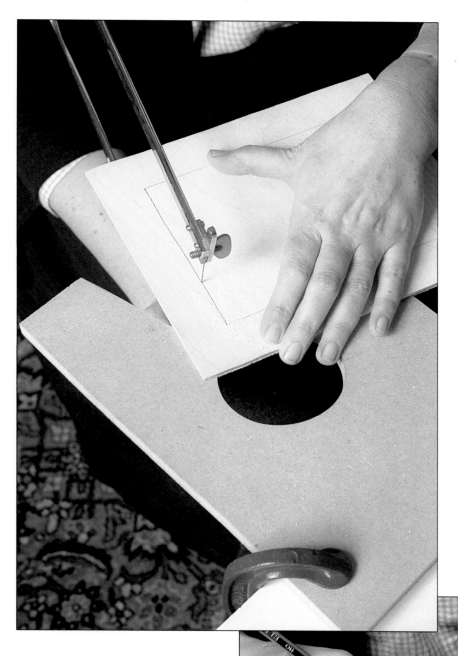

1 Tighten the blade in the frame. Supporting the piece of wood on the keyhole board, cut slowly and evenly along the marked line. With the sandpaper, smooth away any uneveness along the cut edge and tidy up the corners if necessary.

2 The next step is to decorate the frame. Turn it to the right side and lightly draw the design on the wood. This design has been drawn on paper and transferred using carbon paper.

4 Cut a piece of hardboard the same size as the frame to be used as backing, and then cut batten strips to fit the back of this board. You will need three batten strips – two side strips and a bottom strip; the picture will be inserted from the top. Glue the strips to the edges of the backing. Measure between the inner edges of the strips and cut a piece of lightweight card to fit. The picture will be attached to this.

3 Using good quality brushes and paints diluted to a suitable consistency, paint the design on the frame. You may want to practise the technique on the window cut-out first – painting on wood is not difficult, but the surface feels very different from paper.

5 The frame front can now be glued together – if the frame is large, you may want to tap in a few veneer pins from the back.

6 Finally, varnish the whole frame. Build up at least three layers before sanding very lightly with the finest grade of sandpaper. Then add a final coat of varnish.

7 Attach the picture in the correct position to the lightweight card and slide into the completed frame. This frame can be hung or it can be free-standing. To hang, attach screw eyes and picture wire. A sheet of acetate, cut to size, could be inserted in front of the picture to provide a little protection.

8 The wood of the frame and the zebra stripes decorating it emphasize the wildlife setting of the picture.

STAIN FINISH

This frame is made exactly the same way as the one in the previous project; only the style of finish is different. Since the sepia tone of the picture seemed to require a straightforward and unfussy finish, a natural coloured wood stain was used. Other choices for this frame might have been a wood stain in non-wood colours (see page 68) or a thinned wash of paint (see page 70).

E Q U I P M E N T

- as for previous project
- wood stain

P R E P A R A T I O N

Complete the frame as for the preceding project up to the decorating stage.

1 With a clean, soft rag soaked with stain, wipe the surface of the frame. Try to work evenly and quickly so that there will be no 'tide marks' to show the beginning and end of each stroke. Build up the colour with several layers of thinned stain. When you have achieved the right depth of colour, apply varnish to seal the surface.

2 Finish the frame, following steps 4, 5 and 7 in the previous project.

DECOUPAGE FINISH

Follow the same procedure for making this frame as for making the one on page 62; the instructions below are for the finish. To retain the natural quality suggested by the sepia tone of the picture, the natural colour of the birch plywood was maintained. It was embellished with paper cutouts in keeping with the subject of the picture.

EQUIPMENT

■ as for project on page 62
■ scissors
■ tweezers (optional)
■ PVA adhesive
■ paper patterns

PREPARATION

■ Complete the frame up to the decorating stage. Then, decide on the shape of the cut-outs and prepare them. Make sure that their size is appropriate for the width of the frame.
■ Place the cut-out pieces in position on the frame and move around until you are satisfied with the overall appearance. You may wish to mark these positions lightly on the wood.

1 Brush the wrong side of the cut-out pieces with glue. Use the glue sparingly so it will not ooze out at the sides. Removing excess glue without disturbing the other pieces can be difficult.

2 Place one piece in the correct position on the frame using the tweezers if you wish. With a clean, soft cloth, press firmly on the piece being careful not to move it.

3 Fix all the pieces in this way and allow the glue to dry completely.

4 Build up and protect the surface of the frame with at least six coats of varnish. Allow each coat to dry thoroughly before applying the next.

SHAPED WINDOW

The window of this frame is shaped to provide added interest. This type of frame is best used for a picture that is very special and one that will remain in the frame for some time. It could also be used as a gift, but in this case choose a fairly simple shape for the window – a curve or a zig-zag, for example, depending on the effect you want to achieve.

1 First decide on the outer dimensions of the frame and the overall size of the window. Place a piece of tracing paper over the picture; work out the shape of the window and draw it on the tracing paper. Take care not to press so hard with the pencil that the picture is marked.

3 Drill holes through the wood, cut out and complete the frame as in the previous projects, using whichever finish seems most suitable.

EQUIPMENT

- soft pencil
- ruler
- craft knife or scalpel
- cartridge paper
- tracing paper
- lightweight card
- masking tape
- birch plywood (0.6cm or ¼in thick)
- hardboard
- batten strips – as thin as possible
- hand drill
- small saw
- fretsaw
- keyhole board
- clamps
- sandpaper
- wood adhesive
- paint
- brushes
- varnish

2 When the design is ready, transfer the window shape to a piece of cartridge paper and cut out. Place the template on the prepared wood and draw round it.

TIP

The pattern could also be transferred to the wood by drawing over the lines on the reverse side of the tracing paper. Then, with the right side up, place the tracing paper in exactly the right position on the piece of wood and stick down with the tape. Now go over the design and it will be transferred to the surface of the wood.

4 The effect here was achieved using coloured wood stain and varnish.

SHAPED OUTLINE

Both the outline and the window of this frame have been shaped to provide added interest. In this type of frame, the shapes should be chosen to complement, or at least not fight, each other. As a general rule, the window can only be rectangular if the frame has an extended shape (see Figs. 1 and 2). If the outer shape is cut away, the rectangular window looks wrong (see Fig. 3).

EQUIPMENT

- soft pencil
- ruler
- craft knife or scalpel
- cartridge paper
- lightweight card
- masking tape
- birch plywood (0.6cm or ¼in thick)
- hardboard
- batten strips – as thin as possible
- hand drill
- small saw
- fretsaw
- keyhole board
- clamps
- sandpaper
- wood adhesive
- paint
- brushes
- varnish

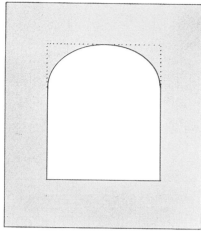

FIG 1

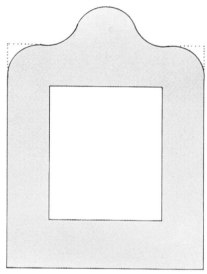

FIG 2

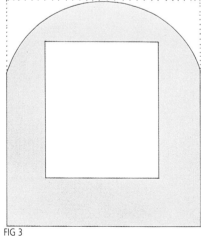

FIG 3

1 Having decided on the overall dimensions of the frame and the size of the window, place a piece of tracing paper over the picture. Draw the dimensions on the tracing paper and work out the chosen shape within these measurements.

2 When the design is ready, draw the outline and window shapes on the piece of paper and cut out a template. Position the template on the prepared piece of wood and draw around the outer outline. Remove the template and cut out the shape. Reposition the template on the shaped piece of wood and draw around the window. Remove the template.

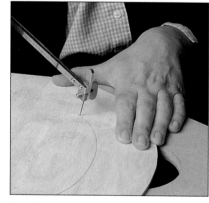

3 Drill holes, insert the blade and cut out the window as for previous projects. When this has been done, complete the frame as before, using whichever finish seems most suitable.

4 For a simple paint wash effect, mix the chosen colour and dilute until the desired intensity is acquired. Test on a piece of scrap plywood.

5 Paint on the wash quickly, stroking on the colour in the direction of the grain.

6 The shape chosen for this frame was determined by the picture itself. The curve echoes the arch of the gateway and is a simple shape to draw and cut.

WOOD FRAMES

BUTTED EDGES

The easiest wooden frame to make is one with butt joints. As this looks quite 'chunky', it is ideal for heavy or thick items such as tiles. The tiles are glued to a base and four strips of wood are nailed to the base around them. Here, compartments have been created for each tile.

This type of frame would also be useful for a piece of tapestry or a painting that is already on a stretcher and does not require glass. Simply cut two strips of wood the height of the painting, and nail them to the sides of

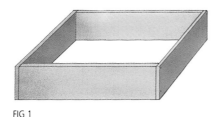

FIG 1

the stretcher. Then cut another two strips the width of the painting plus the side strips and nail them in position, using two nails in each corner (see Fig. 1). The wood strips can be stained or painted and varnished before they are nailed in place.

EQUIPMENT

- ▪ tiles
- ▪ strips of wood
- ▪ wood for base (plywood or similar)
- ▪ ruler
- ▪ pencil
- ▪ tenon saw
- ▪ adhesive suitable for wood
- ▪ moulding pins
- ▪ adhesive suitable for tiles (optional)

PREPARATION

Decide on the arrangement of the tiles and then work out the dimensions of the frame. These tiles are arranged in a square; add the width of the strips of wood to the measurement of the tiles to get the finished size of the base.

1 Lay the tiles on an oversize piece of wood or hardboard. Measure and cut two side strips of wood and the vertical central divider. Place these three strips in position and measure the length of the two remaining outer strips.

2 Cut these and place around the tiles.

3 With the tiles in position, measure and cut the two horizontal dividers.

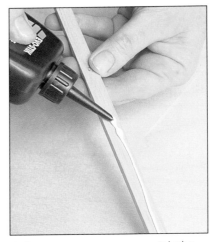

4 Now you can measure accurately the size of the base. Cut the base and glue the strips of wood to the outer edges.

5 Working from the back, mark the position for the pins to secure the outer strips – a distance of half the width of the strip in from the edge.

6 Hammer in the pins. Still working from the underside, mark the position of the dividers – in this case they will be placed centrally. Drill the holes and turn the frame over.

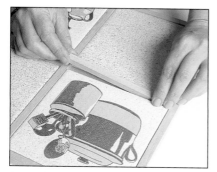

7 Lay the tiles in position and check that the holes are under the dividers. Then glue the dividers in place, remove the tiles and nail from underneath.

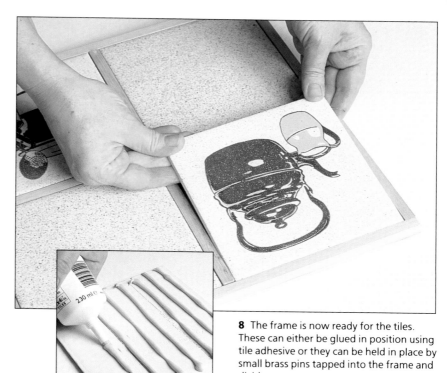

8 The frame is now ready for the tiles. These can either be glued in position using tile adhesive or they can be held in place by small brass pins tapped into the frame and dividers.

9 Varnish or paint the frame as desired. Screw in the hangers.

MITRED JOINTS

This is the most traditional type of frame and in some ways the most difficult to make well. A certain amount of specialized equipment is necessary; this is listed below at the beginning of the project. Some of the tools are general household tools; the specialized framing tools are moderately priced and easily found. For a professional framer, more mechanized equipment is available.

The mitre joint used in picture framing is the weakest type of joint, as compared to dovetail or mortice joints, because it is end to end and for this reason accuracy is essential. There are ways of making this type of frame other than the one used here but the following method is the simplest way of achieving an adequate result with a minimum of equipment.

EQUIPMENT

- sharp pencil
- ruler
- moulding
- mitre box or corner clamp
- saw
- frame clamp
- adhesive suitable for wood
- glass
- glass cutter
- T-square
- moulding pins
- power or hand drill
- tack hammer
- nail set
- wood filler
- stain
- hardboard
- Stanley knife or similar
- brown gummed tape or masking tape

PREPARATION

■ The first step in making the frame is to work out accurately the size of the frame, and from this to calculate the amount of moulding needed. Measure the piece to be framed – this may or may not have a mount. This size will be the measurements of the frame between the rebates (see Fig. 1) plus an allowance of about 0.25cm (⅛in) for ease.

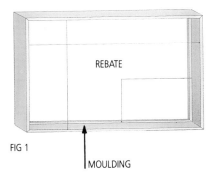

FIG 1

MOULDING

REBATE

■ To calculate how much moulding is needed for a frame, use this formula: add the all-round measurement of the artwork plus eight times the width of the moulding plus a small allowance for cutting (see Figs. 2a and 2b).

■ For the mounted certificate framed here, the amount of moulding required was calculated as follows: the mount measures 40cm × 30cm and the moulding is 2cm wide; 2 × (40 + 30) = 140 + (8 × 2) = 156cm plus cutting allowance of, say 4cm = 160cm; 160cm of moulding was needed.

■ Alternatively, using imperial measurements, the mount measures 15¾in × 11¾in and the moulding is ¾in wide; 2 × (15¾in + 11¾in) = 55 + (8 × ¾) = 61in plus a cutting allowance of 2in adds up to 63in of moulding needed.

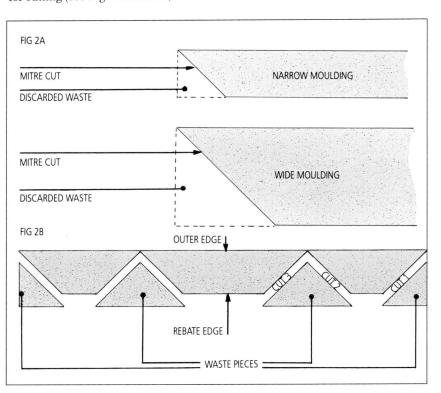

FIG 2A

MITRE CUT

DISCARDED WASTE

NARROW MOULDING

MITRE CUT

DISCARDED WASTE

WIDE MOULDING

FIG 2B

OUTER EDGE

CUT 3

CUT 2

CUT 1

REBATE EDGE

WASTE PIECES

■ If possible, make sure that the mitre box or clamp is fixed to the work surface.

■ If the mitre box is new, use the saw to mark the cross cut on the base so there is a line with which to align the pencil mark.

■ If you are using a new mitre clamp and saw, put a little grease on the surface of the blade to make it run smoothly.

■ Be sure to check that the base of the moulding is flat in the box or clamp before cutting, otherwise the cut will not be vertical and the joins will not fit.

■ If using a clamp, make sure that the pressure of the clamp does not mark the moulding – protect very soft moulding with a piece of card.

■ When cutting a very large frame, it may be necessary to support the moulding that extends beyond the box or clamp on some blocks of wood.

■ When cutting, use the saw smoothly and with light pressure – if you are heavy-handed, the saw will 'jump' and you may get a poor cut.

■ Before gluing the frame together, note that some woods are more absorbent than others and this will affect the amount of glue required and the length of drying time. If possible, try out these properties on some leftover moulding.

■ If the frame is quite deep, pin it together (see step 8) while the frame clamp is still in position and there will be no chance of the join coming undone.

MAKING THE FRAME

■ Prepare to cut one of the long sides of the frame. First, using the corner clamp, cut a mitre at the end of the length of moulding to give a clean edge (see Fig. 2b – cut 1).

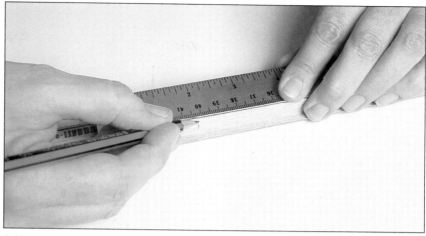

1 Now measure and mark the length of the first long side on the inside of the rebate.

2 Line up the pencil mark on the moulding with the cross-cut in the mitre box or clamp, allowing for the saw cut – a few practice cuts will show how much to allow. Make the second cut – (see Fig. 2b – cut 2) – note the angle of this cut is opposite to the angle of the first.

3 Next, cut off the waste piece (see Fig. 2b – cut 3).

5 Before assembling the frame, rub the cut edges against the rough side of the hardboard to smooth them and then trim off any 'whiskers' with a razor blade or craft knife. Do not use sandpaper as this would rub away too much and affect the fit of the join.

4 Measure the second long side against the piece which has just been cut. On a firm surface, hold the two pieces of moulding back to back and mark the exact length of the first piece on the outside of the moulding; check the measurement with a ruler. Place the moulding in the mitre box or clamp as above and check as before. Then cut the second piece and lay both pieces aside. Repeat the above procedures to cut the two short pieces for the frame. There are now four pieces.

6 Working on a flat surface, lay the pieces close together in the correct positions and place the frame clamp around the outside with the pulling piece on the right-hand side (assuming the framemaker is right-handed). Remove the short pieces and apply glue.

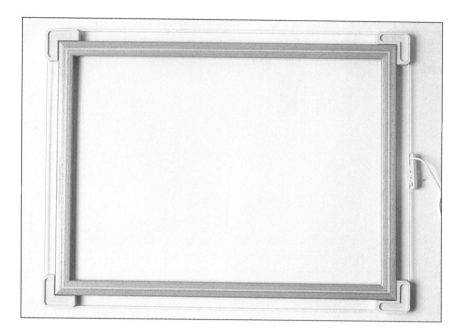

7 Replace the short pieces in their correct positions and tighten the frame clamp by pulling up the cord. When it is really tight, secure it firmly – the cord should 'ping' when pulled. Wipe off any excess glue that has oozed out and set aside to dry for a few hours. Remove the frame clamp and check that there is no excess glue in the rebate. If there is, remove it with a craft knife or razor blade.

8 The frame is now ready to be pinned. The pins will go in more easily if you drill small holes through the moulding for them. Cut off the head of a pin and insert the shaft into the drill as a bit. This ensures that the holes are the right size. If the moulding is narrow, one pin per corner is enough. The pins should be placed in the sides of the frame for strength, but they do show a little. For aesthetic reasons, pins are sometimes placed in the top and bottom pieces.

9 Hammer in the pins using the nail set to drive them below the surface of the wood. Fill the holes with filler and stain to match.

CUTTING THE GLASS

The next stage is to cut the glass. Unless the frame is very large, this is not too difficult. Use a good glass cutter – the more expensive the tool, the better it will be – and take good care of it. Keep the cutting head standing on a rag soaked in household oil diluted with white spirit.

Picture glass is thinner than window glass and quite fragile to handle in sheet form. Try a few practice cuts first. Most people hold the glass cutter between the index and middle finger for good control but this is not essential. Be sure to hold the cutter at a constant angle.

Once you master the glass cutting technique, you are ready to cut the glass to size. The glass should be cut to the same size as the piece of work being framed. When measuring the glass, allow for the cutter's width against the ruler – about 0.25cm (⅛in).

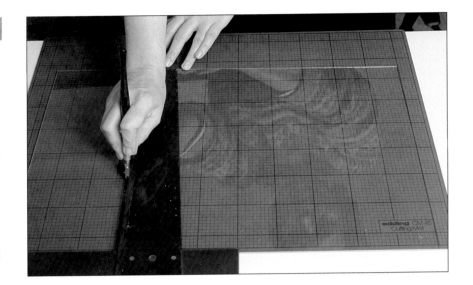

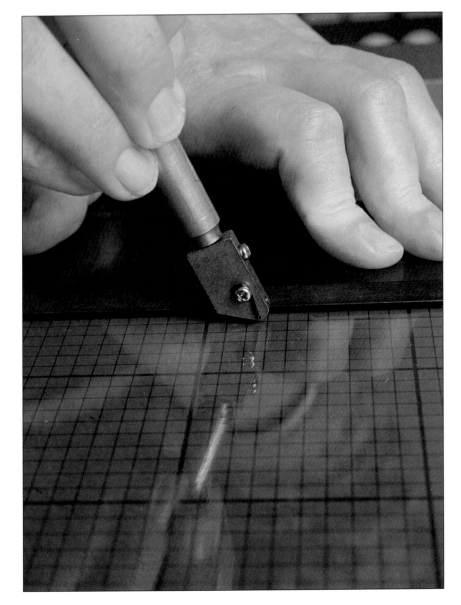

1 Lay the glass so that it overhangs the work surface slightly and position the T-square along its edge. Hold the glass cutter fairly upright and keep the arm extended so that the body moves back rather than the elbow bending.

2 Draw the cutter along the surface of the glass with an even pressure – there should be an audible 'hiss'. Break the glass (see below) and repeat the process for the other dimension.

BREAKING THE GLASS

There are several ways to break the glass after scoring it:

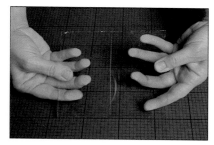

1 Hold the glass in both hands on both sides of the line and press up with the fingers and down with the thumbs.

2 Place the glass on the edge of the work surface with the score line parallel to the edge and press down gently.

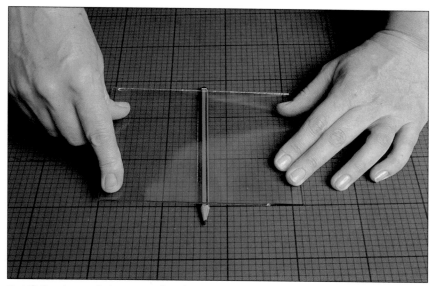

3 Lift the glass and place a pencil under the score line. Press down on both sides.

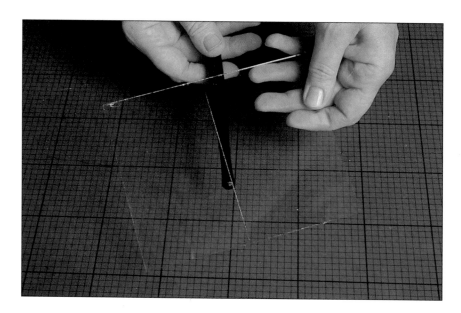

4 Lift the glass and, from underneath, tap along the score line with the end of the cutter.

FINISHING THE FRAME

▌ The hardboard for the backing can be cut to size in almost the same way you cut the glass using a Stanley knife. Draw the knife along the straight edge several times and then break by applying hand pressure.

▌ Fix D-rings to the hardboard or screw rings in the moulding for hanging. If you use D-rings, insert them at this stage. They should be positioned one-third of the way down from the top and 5–8cm (2–3in) in from the sides depending on the size of the frame.

1 Mark the correct position and pierce with a bradawl. Place the D-ring in position and insert the rivet through the hole. Turn over the hardboard and, working on a hard surface, split the rivet and hammer it flat.

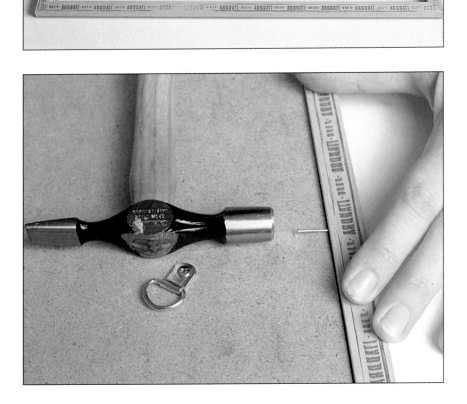

2 All the components of the frame are now ready to assemble. Place the glass in the frame from the back and clean the inside. Next put in the piece of work for which the frame has been made.

3 Put in the hardboard and secure it with a few pins or glazier's points. If you plan to do much framing, you can get a special tool called a point driver.

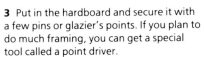

4 Take the tape and stick it to the back of the frame to protect the contents of the frame from the atmosphere.

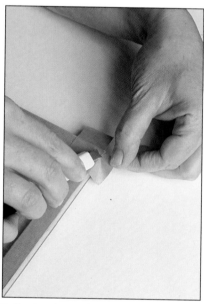

5 Neaten the overlap at the corners for a tidy appearance. If using screw rings, insert them and the wire or cord; the picture is complete.

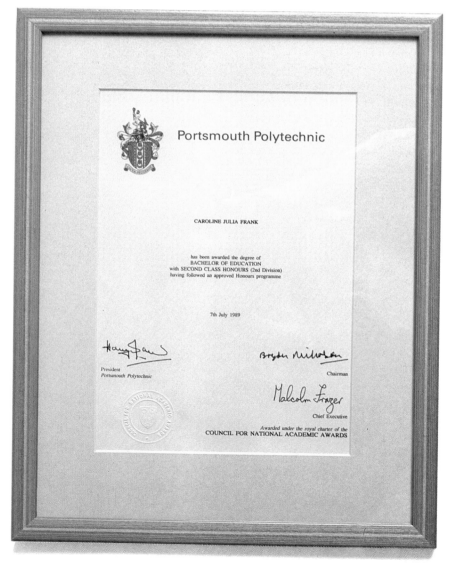

6 With a little practice, truly professional results can be achieved.

MITRED FRAME WITH SLIP LINER

Slip liners or inserts are often used for pictures or articles that require distancing from the frame. They are also used frequently with oil or acrylic paintings and other works that do not require glass. They can be used to create box frames with glass as shown on page 106. Best described as frames within frames, they provide a soft transition from the artwork to the frame and surroundings.

The method for framing this picture is generally the same as that used for the basic mitred frame on page 74. The main difference is that the slip liner should fit into the outer frame snugly – if it stays in place without any glue or pins then this is indeed an excellent job. However, it is quite permissible to secure the slip frame in place with moulding pins if necessary.

EQUIPMENT

- sharp pencil
- ruler
- moulding
- slip liner
- mitre box or corner clamp
- saw
- frame clamp
- adhesive suitable for wood
- moulding pins
- power or hand drill
- tack hammer
- nail set
- wood filler
- stain

COVERING A MITRED FRAME

Slip liners are often covered with material – the one used in this example was purchased as shown. However, if a suitable one cannot be found, you can make your own quite easily using a simple flat or rounded moulding (see Figs. 1–3).

▌ First make up a mitred frame as described in the previous project. Then cover this frame with strips of fabric (see Fig. 1).

▌ Letting the fabric overhang both edges of the moulding, glue in place. Mitre the corners and peel away waste areas A and B (see Fig. 2).

▌ Then glue the fabric neatly into place along the 'sight' edge of the moulding. Trim the other edge flush with the moulding – this will be under the rebate of the outer frame (see Fig. 3).

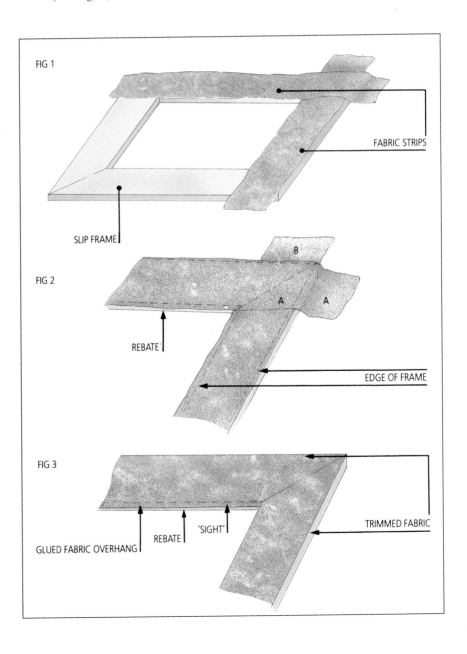

FIG 1

FABRIC STRIPS

SLIP FRAME

FIG 2

B

A   A

REBATE

EDGE OF FRAME

FIG 3

GLUED FABRIC OVERHANG   REBATE   'SIGHT'   TRIMMED FABRIC

PREPARATION

■ The first step is to work out accurately the sizes of the inner and outer frames and, from these measurements, to calculate the amount of liner and moulding needed. Measure the picture and add an allowance of 0.25cm (⅛in) for the inner frame – no allowance is needed on the outer frame.

1 Now make the inner frame following steps 1–6 for the basic mitred frame. However, if the purchased liner is made of cloth, be sure to protect it with masking tape whenever a cut is made – this keeps the cloth from tearing. Proceed as follows:

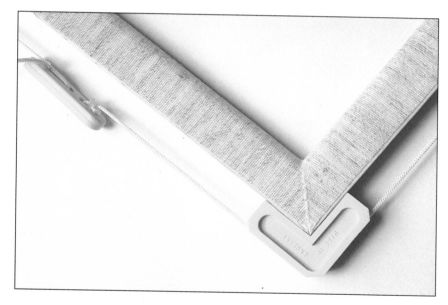

2 Replace the short pieces in their correct positions and tighten the frame clamp by pulling up the cord. When it is really tight (the cord should 'ping' when pulled), secure it firmly. Wipe off any excess glue that has oozed out. Set aside to dry for a few hours. As this 'frame' will be framed, you need not pin it unless it is very deep.

3 Now make the outer frame using the basic mitred frame instructions. You can use the completed inner frame to mark the necessary measurements on the moulding but do not add an allowance.

83

4 When this frame is complete, place the picture into the slip frame and secure with pins.

5 Place this 'frame' in the outer frame. Screw eyes are normally used to hang this type of frame.

6 The slip liner adds a soft edge to the picture and separates it from the frame.

FABRIC
FRAMES

SIMPLE METHOD

This frame can be made in any size depending on the size of the photograph. For larger sizes, however, the proportions may have to be altered. This frame measures 5cm (2in) more than the photograph both in length and in width. Prepare all the parts before starting.

EQUIPMENT

- thin card
- fabric for covering
- fusible webbing
- piece of paper for lining
- pencil
- ruler
- scissors
- craft knife
- glue
- iron
- scrap paper

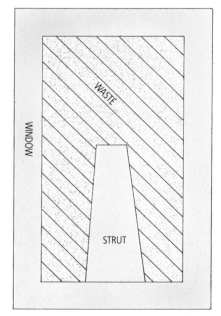

FIG 1

1 Cut two pieces of thin card to the required size. Mark and cut a window in one piece leaving a 2.5cm (1in) border all around. Using the window piece, cut out the strut following the diagram (Fig. 1) as a guide. The strut should be no more than half the height of the frame.

2 Cut two pieces of fabric and fusible paper-backed webbing 3cm (1½in) larger all around than the card frame. Then cut two pieces of fabric for the strut so they overlap the strut by 3cm (1½in) at the top and by 1cm (½in) at both sides and the wide end. Iron the webbing to the wrong side of all the fabric pieces.

3 Peel away the paper from the piece of fabric for the frame back, lay it on the corresponding piece of card and carefully iron in position. Take care not to iron over the edges because the fabric will adhere to the ironing surface.

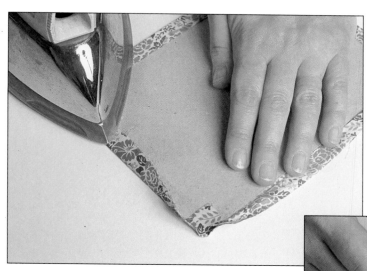

4 To turn in the edges, use the tip of the iron. First work on the frame back. Turn in the four corners and fix down. Then turn in the sides. Pay particular attention to the corner areas to make them as neat as possible.

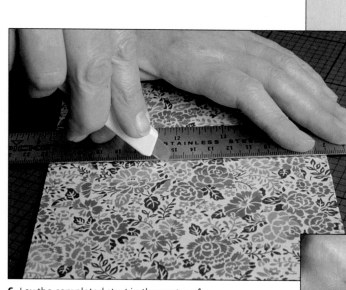

5 Follow the same procedure with the strut piece, but leave the 3cm (1½in) extension at the top free. Lay this on the other piece of strut and draw around it. Cut just inside this line, peel away the backing and iron it into position, including the extension.

6 Lay the completed strut in the centre of the frame back on the fabric-covered side. At this point, you should decide whether the finished frame will be vertical ('portrait') or horizontal ('landscape'). Holding the tab of fabric out of the way, mark the position of the top of the strut. Using the craft knife, carefully cut through the card slightly above this line.

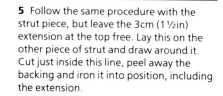

7 Push the tab through this slit, check to make sure the strut is in the correct position, apply glue to the tab and hold down until fixed.

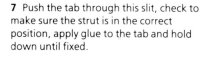

8 Peel away the backing paper from the remaining piece of fabric, carefully position it on top of the card for the frame front and iron in place. Cut out a smaller window 1cm (½in) away from card window but do not discard the fabric.

9 Turn in the outer edges as on the frame back and iron in place.

10 Now clip the excess on the window edges almost into the corners, turn this over to the wrong side and iron into place.

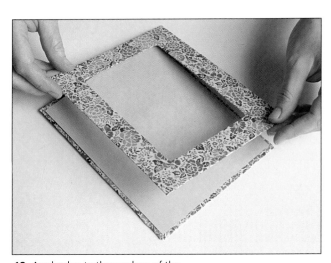

11 Cut the piece of paper so that it is a fraction smaller than the completed back of the frame. Glue this paper onto the wrong side of the fabric-covered back to mask the turned-in edges and tab. It will also help the photograph slide in and out of the frame easily.

12 Apply glue to three edges of the paper-covered back of the frame, leaving the bottom, where the base of the strut is centred, unglued. Carefully position the frame front on top and place under a weight, such as a pile of books, to dry. If you wish, cut a piece of acetate the same size as the photograph and slide it into place with the photograph to protect it.

15 Then place the restraining strap between the strut and the frame back and hold until fixed.

FIG 2

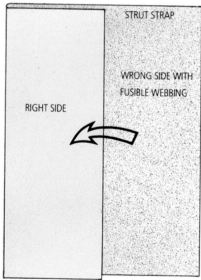

STRUT STRAP

WRONG SIDE WITH FUSIBLE WEBBING

RIGHT SIDE

13 Finally, make a restraining strap to keep the strut in place. Take a small scrap of material – 6cm (2½in) square – from the window cut-out. Peel off the paper backing, fold over one third and press with the iron tip. Fold over the remaining third and press.

FIG 3

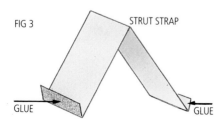

STRUT STRAP

GLUE   GLUE

14 The strap is now 2cm × 6cm (3¼in × 2½in). Fold in half lengthwise and apply glue in a narrow line at both ends.

16 The fabric for the frame can match the decor or reflect the subject of the photograph.

PADDED METHOD

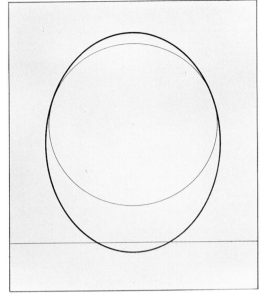

FIG 1

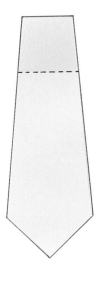

FIG 2

PREPARATION

- Decide whether the frame opening is to be oval or circular. Then cut two pieces of thick card – square if the opening is circular, or rectangular for the oval window (see Fig. 1). Cut one piece of card for the strut (see Fig. 2).
- Make a template: draw a circle using compasses or an oval, using the method described on page 37. Cut out the window.
- Cut two pieces of fabric 2cm (¾in) larger all round than the card pieces and one piece the same size as the card to use as a facing. Also cut one piece which is 1.5cm (¾in) smaller all around than the card pieces; this piece can be cut from contrasting fabric. For the strut, cut two pieces 7cm × 15cm (3in × 6in). Cut two pieces of wadding the same size as the card.

1 Draw around the template onto one piece of thick card.

2 Cut out the window. If the edges of the opening are rough, use the sandpaper to smooth them.

3 Apply glue to both pieces of card and carefully place the wadding on the card. Allow to dry.

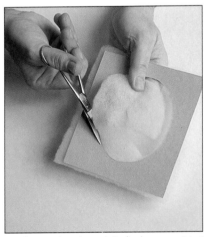

4 Then, using the pointed scissors, cut out the opening.

5 Place the card, wadding side up, on the fabric piece of the same size wrong side up and draw around the opening.

6 Lay this piece of fabric, with the opening drawn on it, in the centre of one of the large pieces with the right sides together. Pin in position and stitch carefully around the drawn line.

7 Cut away the fabric inside the stitching leaving a 0.5cm (¼in) seam allowance.

8 Clip almost to the stitching at regular intervals all round. Turn inside out so the right sides are facing out and press.

9 Pass the facing (the smaller piece) through the opening of the frame front so that it lies against back of the card and the larger piece of fabric covers the wadding on the front.

10 Pin through the seam into the cut edge of the opening, making sure that the clipped seam allowance is on the back or card side.

11 Carefully apply some adhesive around the back of the frame close to the opening, press the seam allowance in position and allow to dry. Glue the rest of the facing in position neatly on the back.

12 Cut strips of double-sided adhesive tape and lay along two of the outside edges of frame. Peel away the backing strips and turn in the corners. Stretching the fabric, turn over the edge and press on to the sticky tape. Now work on the opposite edge.

13 Next lay strips of double-sided adhesive tape along the other two outside edges and turn in the remaining fabric, making the corners as neat as possible. If you are using a thick fabric such as velvet, mitre the corners to avoid excess bulk.

14 Take the piece of card for the back, centre the smaller piece of fabric on it and glue in place. Then take the remaining large piece of fabric and cover the card as above.

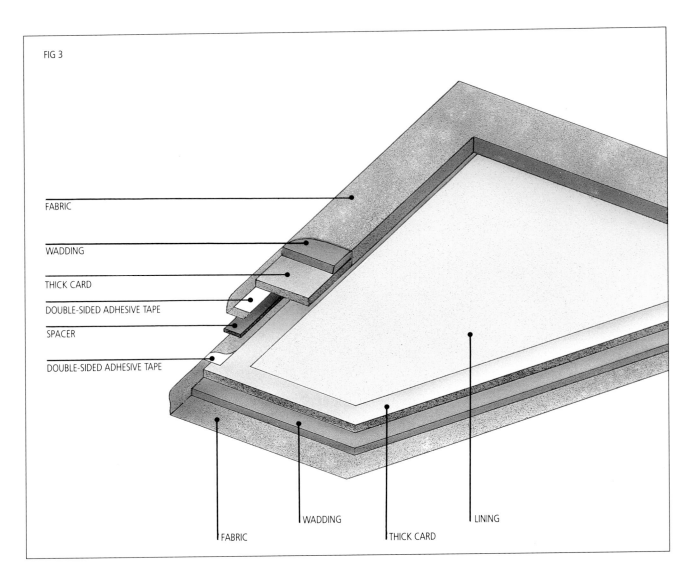

FIG 3

FABRIC

WADDING

THICK CARD

DOUBLE-SIDED ADHESIVE TAPE

SPACER

DOUBLE-SIDED ADHESIVE TAPE

FABRIC

WADDING

THICK CARD

LINING

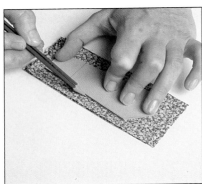

15 From scrap card, cut two strips 0.5cm (½in) wide and as long as the frame and one strip 0.5cm (½in) wide. This strip should be long enough to fit snugly at the top of the frame between the two long strips when they are glued in position just inside the outside edges. These act as spacers.

16 If the frame is to be trimmed with lace it can be inserted at this point. Apply glue to one side of the spacers and press in position on the frame back. Apply more glue to the top face of the spacers and position the completed frame front on top of the frame back (see Fig. 3). Leave to dry under a book so that the frame is under a little pressure.

17 Now lay the strut on one of the pieces of fabric cut for it and draw around it. Place it on top of the other piece with right sides together and stitch along the two long sides and across the top. Leave the pointed end open. Trim away the excess fabric and turn right side out.

18 Take the card piece for the strut and score across the dotted line, being careful not to cut through. Push the card into the fabric case, turn in the edges on the open side and stitch together.

19 Bend the completed strut and place the pointed end in the corner of the back. Apply glue to the bent area and press into position.

20 Slide the picture into the frame from the bottom.

21 The padded frame has a soft look that is especially appropriate for photographs of children.

▌ You can make padded frames in different shapes and sizes, using remnant dress material or light furnishing fabric.

EMBROIDERY-DECORATED

This frame is similar to the padded fabric frame on page 90, but it has a more elaborate shape and embroidered decoration. You can vary the shape and size of the frame if you wish. If the outer edge is curved, cut notches in the fabric so that it turns smoothly – this technique is equivalent to clipping the inside curve of the facing.

EQUIPMENT

- thin card
- fabric for covering
- fusible webbing
- piece of paper for lining
- pencil
- ruler
- scissors
- craft knife
- glue
- iron
- scrap paper
- embroidery thread

PREPARATION

First design the embroidery – it can relate to the picture to be framed or it can be an unrelated design.

Remember that the design and final appearance of the frame should not overpower the picture.

1 Mark the frame area with tacking stitches and decide where the embroidery should be positioned. Transfer the design to the material, using either a pencil or a washable quilter's pen, and begin to work the embroidery.

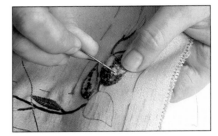

2 In this piece the stem stitch, cretan stitch and french knot were used. Several shades of green thread give depth to the leaves and the stems. If you wish, you can stretch the material on an embroidery hoop.

3 When the embroidery is completed make up the frame following the instructions for the padded frame on page 90.

APPLIQUE-DECORATED

This padded frame is decorated with appliqué. The method and materials used are similar to those in the previous projects. Try to choose a fabric that will complement and blend with the picture to be framed. If the frame is made from a very decorative fabric and an appliqué is added, the picture may be completely overpowered.

The only extra equipment you will need are fabric scraps for the appliqué and fusible webbing.

PREPARATION

▌ First design the appliqué – this can relate to the picture to be framed or it can be an unrelated design.

▌ Mark the frame area with tacking stitches and decide where the appliqué should be positioned.

▌ Iron the fusible webbing on the wrong side of the fabric scraps. Make templates of the shapes and draw the required number of pieces on the paper side of the webbing, cut them out and peel away the backing.

2 Stitch around the edges of the shapes using a sewing machine and zig-zag stitch, if possible.

1 Position the pieces on the fabric for the frame and carefully iron into place.

3 Once decorated, the frame should be made up in the same way as the padded frame on page 90. The shape and colours of the appliqué petals clearly echo the form of the plant in the photograph.

▌ In the example shown here, the material chosen is comparatively plain – the appliqué flower matches the trim of the frame and tones with the clothes worn by the child.

POCKET MIRROR

The mirror used in this project is 7.5cm × 10cm (3in × 4in) but you could use the same procedure to frame a smaller or larger size. If possible, have the edges of the mirror polished so that they are no longer sharp, or rub them down with emery paper.

EQUIPMENT

- thin mirror
- card
- fabric
- fusible webbing
- double-sided adhesive tape
- paper
- pencil
- ruler
- scissors
- craft knife

PREPARATION

- Cut a piece of card the same size as the mirror. Cut a window in this, leaving a frame of 1cm (½in) all around.
- Cut one piece each of fabric and fusible webbing 2.5cm (1in) larger all around than the mirror – in this case 10cm × 12.5cm (4in × 5in). Cut a second piece of each the same size as the mirror. Fuse the fabric pieces to the corresponding webbing pieces.
- Position the card frame front on the fabric and draw around the window. Draw another window 0.5cm (¼in) away within it and cut it out.

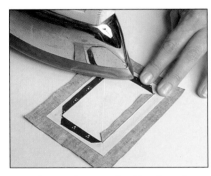

1 Peel away the paper backing from the webbing and use the iron to bond the fabric to the card frame front. Turn in and iron down the window turnings (seam allowance) to the back of the card frame front.

2 Apply small pieces of double-sided adhesive tape to the window turnings on the frame front.

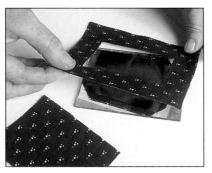

3 Peel away the tape backing and press the frame front on to the mirror.

4 Cut a piece of paper the same size as the mirror and stick it to the back with double-sided adhesive tape. Then turn in the outer fabric edges and iron to bond.

5 Now iron the remaining piece of fabric on to the back of the mirror to give a neat finish.

6 Pocket mirrors make excellent gifts.

MULTIPLE FRAMES

HINGED WOOD FRAMES

Two or three related pictures can be framed in identical frames, and these can then be hinged together with appropriate metal hinges. In the example shown here two small posters, framed in simple moulding, have been joined with small brass hinges.

EQUIPMENT

- as for basic mitred frame (see page 74)
- small brass hinges
- bradawl
- brass screws
- small screwdriver

PREPARATION

- The method for making these frames is exactly the same as for the basic mitred frame (see page 74).
- In making an identical pair of frames, it is a good idea to keep the pieces for each apart – it is very unlikely that the four pieces measured and cut by hand for each frame will be exactly the same.
- When the two frames are complete, lay them side by side and decide on the position of the hinges. Placing them is done by eye – as a rough guide, divide the frame edge into quarters and place one hinge at the bottom of the top quarter and the other hinge at the top of the bottom quarter (see Fig. 1).

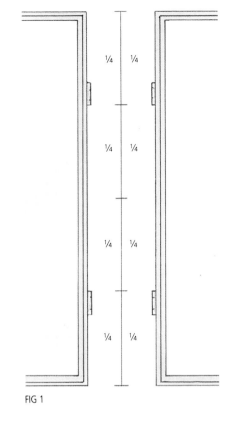

¼ ¼

¼ ¼

¼ ¼

¼ ¼

FIG 1

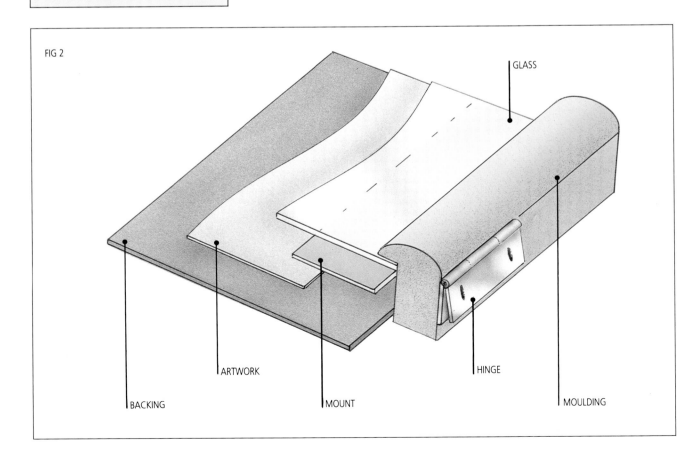

FIG 2

GLASS

BACKING

ARTWORK

MOUNT

HINGE

MOULDING

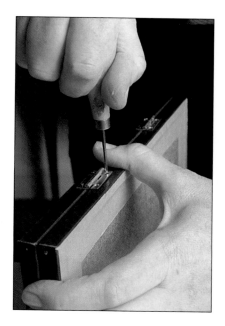 

1 Now, using the bradawl, mark the actual position of the hinges on the first frame and screw in place. Be sure to get the hinges in the correct place on the frame moulding so that the frames will open and close (see Fig. 2). To achieve this, the pin of the hinge must protrude at the front of the moulding so that movement is unimpeded.

2 Stand the two frames in the closed position on a firm surface – if the bottom edges are not level, the frames will not stand properly when they are joined. With the bradawl, mark the holes for the other half of the hinge and screw together.

3 The hinged frames link the two pictures and make them free-standing.

MULTI-MOUNTS

It is possible to buy ready-cut mounts with one or more windows; a few examples are shown on the facing page. If these are not suitable, you can design and cut your own.

EQUIPMENT

- selected mountboard
- ruler
- pencil
- large piece of paper
- scrap paper
- circle cutter
- craft knife or scissors
- fine sandpaper
- masking tape

The photographs on this page show several generations of one family; they are mounted in a simple family-tree formation to show the relationships. As the windows are quite small and show only the heads, they were cut with a circle cutter and therefore have no bevel (professional framers have machinery to cut ovals and circles with bevels). Rectangular windows in a multi-mount could be cut in the usual way.

1 This kind of project needs careful planning; use a large piece of paper to decide on the positions and then work out the overall size of the mount.

2 If the windows are all to be the same size, you can cut out a template with a window, and use it to trim the photographs.

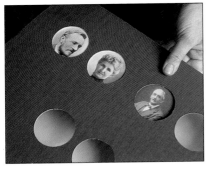

4 When you have cut all the windows from the mountboard and smoothed away any slight unevenness with sandpaper, you can fix the photographs in position with masking tape.

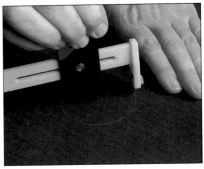

3 Allow plenty of space and time to cut out the windows to minimize errors. You would not want to have to mark out and cut the windows more than once!

5 Here, the names were written using calligraphy on paper that tones with the mountboard and glued beneath the appropriate photograph to give an overall unity to the piece.

6 All the faces, names and relationships show clearly in the finished picture.

READY-CUT MULTI-MOUNTS

The postcards displayed in this nine-window mount came from various places, but they are all related. Framed together, they show an interesting and slightly unusual use of this type of mount.

1 Multi-mounts come in a variety of sizes and have differing numbers of windows.

2 Select the mount that comes closest to your needs – in this case one with many windows of various shapes for the different types of pictures to be framed.

3 Each picture was fitted to the most appropriately sized and shaped window to make a balanced whole.

DOUBLE FABRIC FRAMES

This double, free-standing padded frame is made in almost the same way as the basic padded frame (see page 90).

(see page 90)

EQUIPMENT

- thick card
- thin card
- scrap card for templates or template plastic
- fabric for covering
- fusible webbing and interfacing
- wadding
- double-sided adhesive tape
- glue suitable for fabric
- pencil
- ruler
- scissors with points
- craft knife
- pins, needle and thread
- sandpaper or emery board
- braid or piping for trimming (optional)
- sewing machine (optional)

PREPARATION

■ Begin by preparing all the materials. Cut four pieces of card to the required size; two of these will need windows. You will also need a narrow (1cm – ½in) strip of card the same length as the frame.

■ Cut two pieces of fabric to cover the fronts and two pieces as backing for the two frame fronts – the backs can contrast if you wish. Cut the wadding for the frame fronts only at this stage.

■ The fabric for the outside of the frame should be twice the width of one frame as it covers both the frames (see Fig. 1). The outside could be made from the same contrasting fabric you use to back the frame fronts.

■ A hinge piece is also required – this should be the same length as the frame and 7cm (2½in) wide. One piece of fusible interfacing and one piece of fusible webbing should be cut to this size.

FIG 1

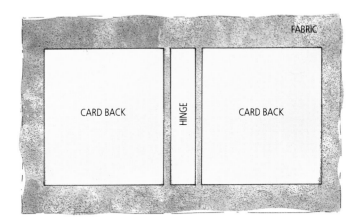

CARD BACK   HINGE   CARD BACK   FABRIC

1 Make the two frame fronts as for the basic padded frame (see page 90).

2 Take the piece of fusible interfacing and mark the centre. Lay the strip of card on this line. Draw lines 1cm (½in) away from the strip on both sides. Position the two frame backs against these lines with the interfacing on top of the card. Iron in place. Lay the card strip in the centre of the interfacing and iron.

3 Now measure this hinged piece and cut a piece of wadding to fit. Glue it to the outside.

4 Trim away the excess wadding – the interfacing should still be visible.

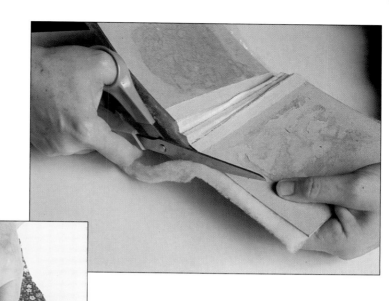

5 Next cover the frame back using double-sided adhesive tape. Taking particular care with the centre hinged area, turn in the top and bottom edges first. Then turn in the sides making sure not to pull them so tight that the frame will not close.

6 Take the piece of webbing and iron it on to the fabric piece of the same size.

7 Peel away the backing and fuse in place down the centre of the frame to cover the card hinge.

8 Now glue the small pieces of backing fabric in place on the hinged frame back.

9 Complete the frame as for the basic padded frame, following steps 15 and 16 (see page 92).

10 The openings in these frames should be along the inside central edges close to the hinge.

11 The completed frame links the two photographs and enables them to stand.

BOX
FRAMES

105

WOODEN FRAMES

Some pieces of work to be framed are three dimensional. There are several ways to deal with this challenge – some are more complicated than others.

First, consider the depth of the object to be framed. Some embroidery, for example, could be accommodated by the addition of foam board or a double or triple mount (see pages 38 and 41).

If the object is deeper, you might use two frames and place the glass between them (see Fig. 1). The inner frame, for the object, could be made from a slip-style moulding such as the one used for the landscape painting on page 82. The outer frame, with a deeper rebate, would hold the glass,

the inner frame and the backing board with the object mounted on it. This method works well, but it can be expensive as it means making and paying for two frames. Also, mouldings with deep rebates can be hard to find. You can make these quite easily, however, from half-round moulding and batten strips. These should be glued together and taped while drying (see Fig. 2).

A cheaper way to frame a three-dimensional object is to make a box for it and then frame the box. Various decisions need to be made before starting this type of project:

1 How will the work be fixed to the backing board? Some items, such as stones or paper or dried flowers could be glued; medals could be pinned or attached with Velcro for easy removal.
2 Will the backing board be lined? If so, this can be done with material or paper.

FIG 2

3 Is a mount required? If so, cut in the normal way and then place on top of the box and accommodate within the frame in the usual way.

E Q U I P M E N T

- thick cardboard or wooden strips (see below)
- frame moulding
- backing board
- hardboard
- mount (optional)
- lining (optional)
- impact adhesive for cardboard or adhesive suitable for wood
- tools to make a basic mitred frame (see page 74)

P R E P A R A T I O N

▌ The size of the work to be framed will determine whether cardboard or wood strips should be used for the box. If the piece is larger than 20cm × 30cm (8in × 10in) it is probably wiser to use wood.

▌ Decide on the size of the box and cut two strips of your chosen material the exact width and two strips the length, minus two thicknesses of wood or card (see Fig. 3). Cut the cardboard for the base to size.

▌ The following project uses a cardboard box lined with dark velvet to offset the piece of silver jewellery. The sloping panels are not essential, but they create shallower planes to which a lining, such as velvet, can be attached.

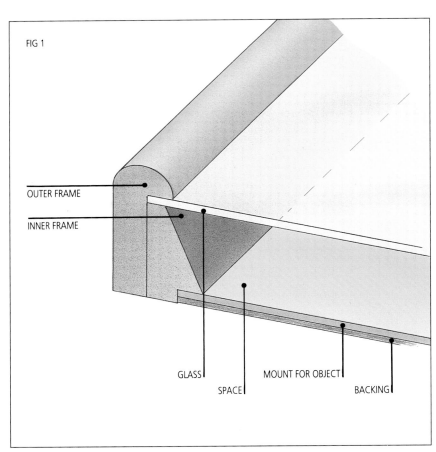

FIG 1

OUTER FRAME

INNER FRAME

GLASS

SPACE

MOUNT FOR OBJECT

BACKING

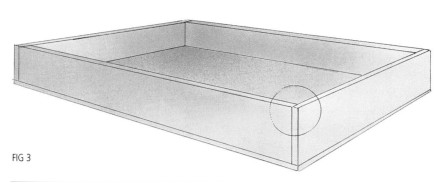

FIG 3

1 Stick the two shorter strips to the corresponding sides of the base, using the appropriate adhesive. Then stick the remaining two strips in position on the other two sides of the base. The box is now finished. If using wooden strips, secure with small pins as well, if wished.

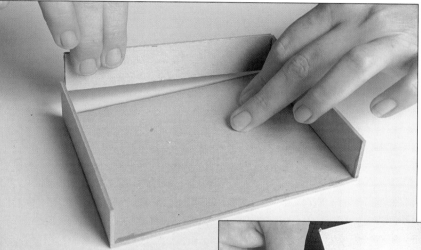

2 Draw a rectangle in the base of the box to define the flat area where the piece of jewellery will lie. Take a piece of card to fit the width of the box and lay it against the line and touching the top edge of the box – this will give the depth of the card. Cut two pieces this size.

3 Now cut two more pieces the same depth but this time the length of the box. Place each panel, in turn, in position against the line drawn in the base in the box and mark each corner point. Cut from these marks to the top corner edges.

107

4 Stick the four panels in position.

5 Cut a piece of velvet almost twice the size of the box. Apply glue sparingly to the card and, starting from the centre, stick the velvet in position. The natural give in the material will accommodate the slopes.

6 Trim away the material so that there is just enough to stick down along the outside edges of the box. Cut the corners neatly.

7 Make a basic mitred frame using the deep moulding. Make sure the allowance on the frame moulding is not forgotten when cutting as the velvet will take up some space. When glueing deep mouldings it is helpful to use two frame clamps while the glue is drying.

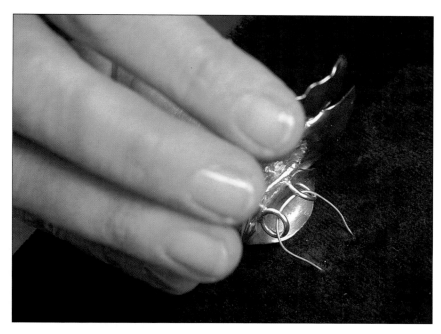

8 Centre the piece of jewellery in the box and pierce two holes through the velvet and cardboard close to the fixing point. Thread a short piece of brass wire through one hole, wrap around the fixing on the back of the jewellery, and return to the back of the box and twist several times.

9 Place the glass on top of the box with the jewellery fixed securely. Lower the frame carefully into position. Turn over and tape the box and frame together as usual.

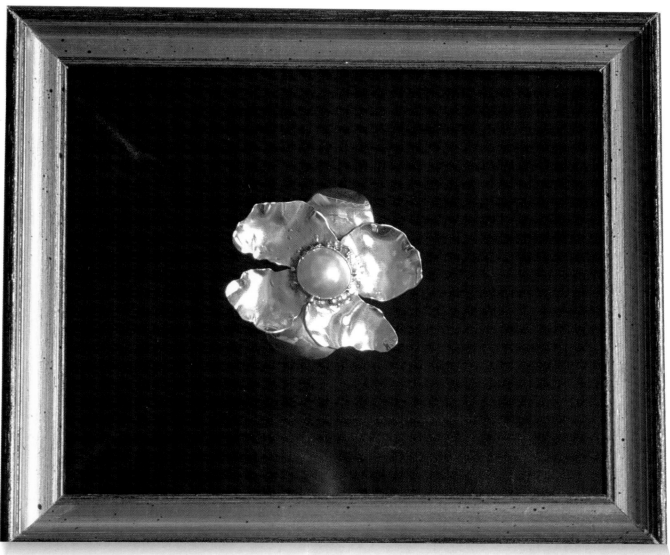

PERSPEX FRAMES

A quicker and simpler way to frame a small, three-dimensional piece of work is to purchase a ready-made perspex box frame and adapt it to accommodate the piece. This might be embroidery, coins, origami or anything that is half the thickness of the frame or less. If the work is deeper, one of the other methods described should be used to ensure that the piece can be fixed firmly enough to hold it.

You can sometimes buy perspex frames that have an insert especially designed to provide a space (see Fig. 1). The standard perspex box frame is shown in Fig. 2. If the first frame is not available, a standard frame can be converted as follows:

EQUIPMENT

- perspex box frame
- pencil
- metal ruler
- craft knife or scalpel
- mediumweight card
- adhesive suitable for card

PREPARATION

- Remove the existing card insert from the frame.
- Take the internal measurements of the frame as accurately as you can. Draw a rectangle of this size on to the card, less an allowance for the thickness of the card.
- Decide on the depth you need for the work to be framed. Add this measurement to each side of the rectangle.
- Now add glue flaps to the edges (see Fig. 3).

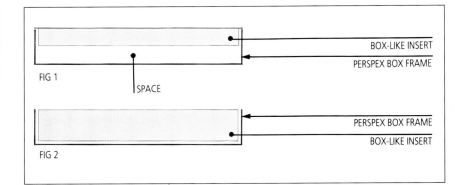

FIG 1
BOX-LIKE INSERT
PERSPEX BOX FRAME
SPACE

FIG 2
PERSPEX BOX FRAME
BOX-LIKE INSERT

FIG 3   GLUE FLAPS A TO POSITIONS B

1 Cut out this shape. Score all the dashed lines by ruling along them with the back of the knife.

2 Now measure the overall size of the frame and cut a piece of card this size. Cut at least two finger holes so you will be able to pull it away from the perspex.

3 Bend all the scored lines; apply glue to the side flaps and glue in position.

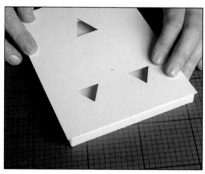

4 Apply glue to the outer, and larger, flaps and position the box centrally on the piece of card – there will be a small overlap all round which will stop the insert from sliding too far into the frame.

5 Fix the work to be framed to a piece of card and then fix this on the box insert with double-sided adhesive tape or glue and place in the frame. You could add a mount supported by strips of foam board if you wished.

6 The box shape leaves plenty of room for the work to float; the clear frame lets in light and enhances the three-dimensional quality.

FLOATING AND PLATFORM FRAMES

Sometimes you may wish to frame a piece of work so that it appears to float instead of being enclosed in a frame. There are three main ways to achieve this effect:

1 Sandwich the artwork between two sheets of glass and use clips or tape to hold the pieces together. This shows both the back and front of the work.

2 Frame the work with a moulding that creates a visible groove between the image and the edge of the frame (see Figs. 1a and b). The groove should appear dark to strengthen the illusion of floating; the inside edge of the moulding may need to be painted a dark colour.

3 Mount the work in such a way that it appears to float on the surface of the backing and then frame the whole (see Fig. 2).

The last two methods are only suitable for works that do not need to be protected from exposure to light and air as they are unglazed and, usually, unsealed.

In the example shown here, the third method is used.

EQUIPMENT

- batten
- sheet of wood
- covering fabric
- staple gun and staples
- screws
- hand drill
- screwdriver
- wood adhesive
- moulding
- tools to make a basic mitred frame (see page 74)

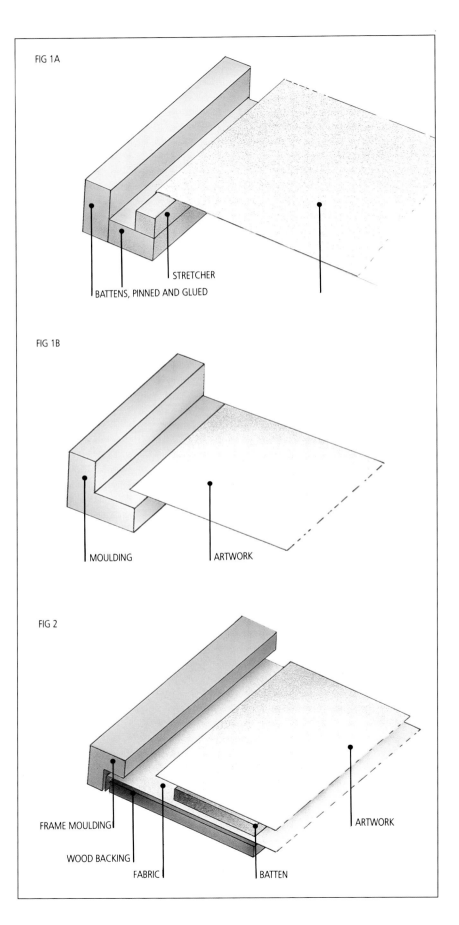

FIG 1A

STRETCHER
BATTENS, PINNED AND GLUED

FIG 1B

MOULDING   ARTWORK

FIG 2

FRAME MOULDING
WOOD BACKING
FABRIC   BATTEN   ARTWORK

MAKING THE BACKING BOARD

1 Cut two strips of batten about 6cm (2½in) shorter than the width of the picture and glue them to the back of the picture, 3cm (1in) from the top and the bottom and equidistant from the sides.

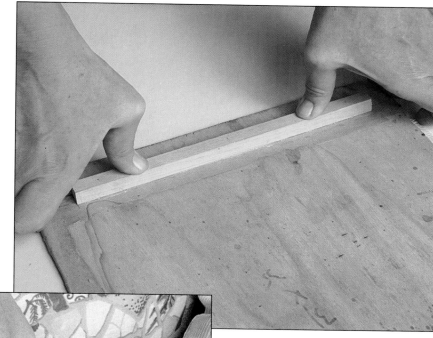

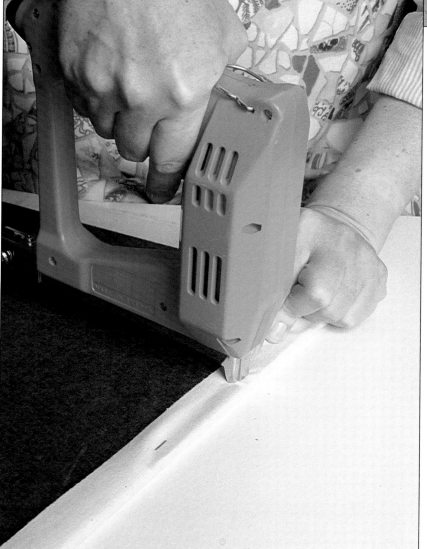

2 Next cut the sheet of wood to the required size and cover it with the chosen fabric. Here, the wood is 50cm × 40cm (20in × 16in) and the fabric is calico which tones with the background of the painting. The fabric has been tightly stretched and stapled to the back of the wood.

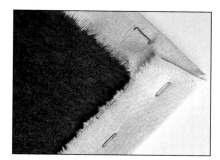

3 Tuck in the corners and staple as neatly as possible.

SECURING THE ARTWORK

With the fabric side down, position the picture on the wood and calculate the position of the holes to secure it by measuring the distance from the lower edge of the wood to the lower edge of the picture. Add the 3cm (1in) to the lower edge of the batten and add half the width of the batten. This gives the position for the lower holes – one in the centre and one at each end. The upper holes should be marked in the same way.

1 Drill the holes through the wood and mark these with a nail on the battens. Then drill guide holes into the battens to receive the screws.

2 Countersink the drill holes so that the wall is not damaged by protruding screws once the picture is hung.

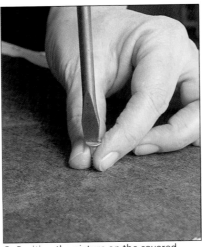

3 Position the picture on the covered surface of the wood and screw through from the back to secure it using flat-head screws.

4 Now make a mitred frame for this 'picture' in the usual way (see page 74). It will not be necessary to cut glass for this frame or to seal the back. The picture is fixed into the frame with hardboard corners on the back because the moulding has a narrow rebate; the fabric-covered board fits flush into it allowing no space for pins.

5 This oil painting had been worked on a rough piece of wood in a spontaneous way; a conventional frame would have hemmed it in and would not have extended the feeling of space inherent in the painting.

READY-MADE FRAMES

METAL FRAMES

Metal frames in a variety of sizes and finishes are now available in many shops; they can also be ordered in special sizes.

The photo-collage shown here has a very simple red metal frame which complements the piece of work. As it is a very large piece measuring 81cm × 112cm (32in × 44in), glass would have made the frame excessively heavy. The glass-substitute used instead is much lighter in weight, but it is easily scratched and attracts static. In price, they are about the same.

If the metal frame comes unassembled, a pack containing all components needed to assemble it will be supplied. This will contain corner pieces, screws, clips to keep the backing in position and hangers. The glass, or glass-substitute if you want to use it, and the backing must be purchased separately. You may be able to order them from the frame supplier.

Gather together all the parts of the frame, the piece to be framed, a mount if you are using one, and the wire. The only equipment you will need is a screwdriver and a pair of pliers.

1 Take one short piece for the frame and two corner pieces, slide them into position and screw up but do not tighten.

2 Take the two long pieces for the frame and slide them into position at right angles to the short piece with the corner brackets. Screw up these corners checking to make sure the mitres are as neat as possible before tightening.

3 Take the second short piece, insert the other two corner pieces and screw up but do not tighten. Leave on one side. If using glass, clean the inside. If using glass-substitute, peel away the protective covering from both sides. With the frame flat and front side down, slide the glass or substitute into position.

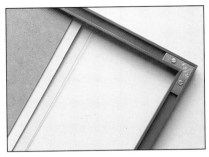

4 Next, slide the piece of work, with its mount if used, into position, image side down. Finally, slide the backing into the frame. If the hangers are of the sliding type, put them in at this stage but do not tighten.

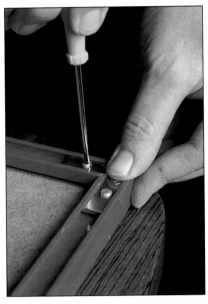

5 Take the remaining short piece, with the attached corner pieces and slip into place on the frame. Making sure that all the layers – glass, picture and backing – are in the groove, screw up and tighten.

6 Place the spring clips evenly around the back of the frame to keep everything firmly in place.

7 Secure the hangers in position approximately one quarter to one third of the way down the frame and attach the picture wire.

8 The metal frame adds a narrow border and is an easy option for a simple frame.

WOODEN FRAMES

A large selection of ready-made wooden frames is available; several alternatives are shown here. These frames can be useful, but the range of sizes available in ordinary shops tends to be limited.

If you want a large or unusual size, go to a specialist framing shop where you will have a greater choice and can order the size you need.

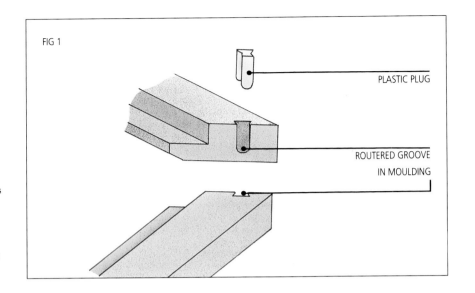

FIG 1

PLASTIC PLUG

ROUTERED GROOVE
IN MOULDING

■ The silkscreen print shown here needed very careful framing because of its vibrant colours. It is printed right to the edge of the paper and has therefore been mounted on a larger piece of background paper to emphasis the technique. The blue moulding is perfect for the picture and shows that colour is as important as shape when choosing a frame.

The most modern way to put together a wooden frame is to use plastic plugs to join mitres which have been shaped to form a type of dovetail joint (see Fig. 1). Some professional framers now use this method in addition to the traditional underpinned method.

When choosing ready-made frames make sure to have the artwork on hand so you can choose a frame that will show both picture and frame to their best advantage.

■ Ready-made wooden frames come in a wide variety of finishes to go with almost any decor; some include mounts. This selection features painted, veneered and antique-gold finishes.

CLIP FRAMES

Clip frames are probably the cheapest of all ready-made frames and, if properly used, can look extremely attractive. They come in a vast number of sizes and in several styles.

Sometimes a piece of artwork can be sandwiched in place in a clip frame and hung. If you want to embellish the artwork, however, choose a clip frame at least one size larger than necessary and mount the work in one of the ways described in the chapter on Mountboard Frames (see page 27).

3 Clip frames allow a very clean, uncluttered effect.

1 This piece of calligraphy has a lovely deckled edge which would be hidden if it was mounted in the usual way. For this reason the piece was mounted on a toning piece of mountboard.

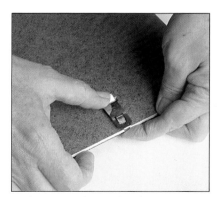

2 The mounted artwork is then sandwiched in the clip frame.

■ A number of different type of clips can be used to hold the clear front of the frame to the backing. Some are shown here.

APPENDIX

In prehistoric times pictures did not have frames – people painted directly onto the walls of their cave dwellings. Even when ancient civilizations began to construct freestanding buildings of a permanent nature – stone dwellings and places of worship – they continued to decorate the walls. One form of wall painting, the fresco, was made on wet plaster. For centuries, paintings – which usually took the form of icons and other religious works – were often painted directly onto wood panels and remained unframed. In medieval times, the frame was still physically a part of the picture, although the border surrounding a painting might be decorated separately. The illuminated borders, painstakingly crafted by monks to enclose pages of beautifully lettered text, are one example.

The first recorded frames appeared around the 13th century and were made to enclose the dominant form of painting of that period – religious works – and were made for churches and cathedrals, usually by the same craftsmen who designed and made the pulpits and choir stalls. These frames often took the form of a triptych – three panels of wood hinged together; the central panel held the main painting and the two side panels contained a design or painting complimentary to it. As most early frames were designed to 'house' pictures which were grandiose and ecclesiastical in their nature and setting, they frequently used architectural elements. One popular style, the Tabernacle frame, incorporated pilasters and half columns.

In the 15th century, the Renaissance in Italy brought great changes in art and framing. Painters began to see themselves as artists in their own right rather than their employers' servants and saw the frame as an important element in the pictures they were engaged in creating. Frames also became a practical necessity for transporting paintings (frequently portraits which were particularly popular at this time) commissioned by wealthy patrons. As artists became more respected and busier, they had less time to make their own frames; this task passed to the apprentice under the direction of the painter. In this way, the separate craft of framing came into being.

The changes that began in Italy spread to other parts of Europe, but each country developed its own

Above These cave paintings in Tanzania are thought to date from after the prehistoric period, but are typical in that their creators chose to depict scenes from everyday life – hunting, the ever-important search for food, being a predominant subject. Not bounded within a frame, the images almost appear as a moving tableau.

particular character. Although carved frames still predominated, decorative finishes such as marbling, gilding and even the use of fabrics like silk were incorporated.

Under strong French influence in the 17th century, frames became the province of designers rather than artists. Paintings were seen as part of the interior decoration, and furniture designers became the major frame-makers; again, each country developed its own style. Many frames were mass-produced and some of the individuality was lost, although the standard of work remained high.

In the late 17th and early 18th centuries, frames became increasingly ornate, first in the Baroque style and then the Rococo style. Making these elaborate frames required a high degree of skill, and cabinet-makers contracted the work out to specialist carvers. Gradually, the popularity of these extravagant styles waned, and there was a return to simpler, more austere frames. Towards the end of the 18th century, geometric mouldings again became fashionable. At this time, the Adam brothers were at work in England and their style became a major influence. Once again the frame was seen as an integral part of the picture and was specially designed to enhance it.

At the beginning of the 19th century 'composition' frames were introduced and began to replace the traditional carved wood as a material. Resin was set in specially carved moulds and, once the technique had been mastered, frames could be produced much more quickly and less expensively than individually carved frames. Another new technique involved plaster mouldings applied to wood bases, but this was not always successful as the plaster tended to flake off over a period of time. This technique did enable frame-makers to copy old frames more easily, however, and during the Victorian period many

old frames were copied, which heralded a return to more ornate styles.

Towards the end of the 19th century, artists once again became more independant of their clients. They became extremely interested in the way their works were displayed and looked upon the frame as an important part of the whole; this attitude continues to this day. At the same time, many interior designers like to present art as part of the decor and they choose pictures to blend with the whole rather than for their own merit. An interesting development at present is the upsurge in value of old frames; some bring more at auction than the pictures they contain.

The history of picture framing, like so much else in history, is cyclical; styles come and go, and return again. This brief synopsis may help you to identify these different styles – in museums, art galleries or auction rooms – and help you to assess your own pictures and frames with a little more understanding.

Above *Madonna and Child,* Duccio di Buoninsegna. Painted in tempera on a white gesso ground, with lavish application of gold leaf, this triptych is typical of religious works of the 15th century. Note that the painted sections of the wooden panels are slightly recessed and are effectively 'framed' by the raised edges.

Left This modern abstract screenprint required a simple, modern frame and the choice of colour, size and mounting materials serve to enhance the whole.

GLOSSARY

Acid-free: This term describes mountboards and card that do not contain acid. Acid can damage paper and, if used in framing materials, can transfer to the artwork. Acid-free mountboard should have an alkaline pH content of 7.5 to 9.5.

Architrave: A type of moulding used mainly around doors and windows.

Awl: A pointed hand tool used to pierce wood so that screws or pins can be inserted more easily.

Batten: A thin strip of wood used to cover joints or to provide a surface for fixing tiles.

Beading: A narrow strip of shaped material, usually wood, that is used for edging.

Bevel: A sloped edge, usually cut to form the inside edge of a window mount.

Block mount: A piece of wood or blockboard on which a piece of artwork has been mounted.

Box frame: A deep frame designed to display a three-dimensional piece of work.

Bradawl: A pointed hand tool used to pierce wood so that screws or pins can be inserted more easily.

Clip frame: A simple frame consisting of a sheet of glass, a piece of hardboard, and special clips to hold them together. The artwork is sandwiched between the two layers.

Cold mounting: A method of fixing a piece of artwork to a backing using a spray adhesive. It is also known as wet mounting.

Conservation board: This is a mountboard made from rag pulp or from specially treated acid- and chemical-free wood pulp. It is used in the framing of valuable pieces of artwork.

Double mount: Two mounts used together to give a more decorative effect. The top mount has a larger window than the lower mount. This technique is also used to provide a deeper space for work that is slightly raised.

Dry mounting: A method of fixing a piece of artwork to a backing by inserting a special film between them and applying heat. The heat causes the film to dissolve and the two layers to adhere. This process is also known as hot mounting.

Fillet: A strip of wood or plastic which is sometimes used to make space between a piece of art and the glass covering it. Occasionally, it is used purely for decoration. It can also be placed between the liner (see below) and the art.

Floating frame: A method of framing a piece of art, usually an oil painting, so that it appears to float against the background. This is done by creating a recess between the painting and the frame.

Glass: The glass most suitable for picture frames is 2mm ($\frac{1}{12}$in) thick. Non-reflective glass has a finely dimpled surface and is more expensive.

Glass cutter: A special tool for cutting glass. There are two types available: one has a steel wheel; the other has a diamond tip.

Glaze: To cover with glass or to apply a layer of varnish.

Gouache: Opaque watercolour paint in which the pigments are bound with glue. The lighter tones are extended with white. This medium is traditionally used for coloured washes on decorative mounts.

Hinge mount: The traditional way to mount an original piece of work on paper – the window mount is fixed to the backing with a paper hinge; the artwork is fixed to the backing.

Hot mounting: See dry mounting.

Liner: Another name for a slip frame (see slip liner).

Liming wax: A special white paste mix which gives a 'limed' effect when rubbed into wood. It is particularly effective on oak and on stained, open-textured wood mouldings.

Marbling: The process of decorating paper or wood to resemble the mottled appearance of marble. Marbled papers may be used to decorate mounts.

Marquetry: A pattern of inlaid veneers of wood. Mouldings with this form of decoration can be purchased.

Mitre: A right-angle joint or join formed by two pieces of moulding (or card or fabric), each cut at a 45° angle. This type of joint is most often used in picture framing.

Mitre box: A wooden or metal guide to aid in the cutting of wood for mitred corners.

Moulding: A decoratively shaped strip of wood or other material. Mouldings made for framing have a rebate to hold the glass, artwork and backing, but builders' mouldings can be used if a rebate is added.

Mount: A piece of card surrounding a picture. It can protect and enhance the work and has many variations.

Origami: The art of paper folding. It originated in Japan.

Perspex: A rigid plastic in sheet form which is sometimes used instead of glass in picture frames. It is lighter than glass and unbreakable, but it does scratch easily.

Quadrant: A strip of wood shaped like a quarter of a circle that is used to form a rebate.

Rebate: The step or recess in the back of a piece of moulding into which all the parts of the picture are fitted.

Ruling pen: A pen with two parallel, adjustable blades. These are filled with ink or watercolour and used to draw decorative lines on mounts. Some mechanical pens of a fixed width can be purchased.

Score: To mark a line on glass or card with a cutting tool. Scoring glass allows it to be severed; scoring card allows it to be bent neatly. Neither material is cut through when scoring.

Screw eyes: Screws with a ring at the top. They are attached to the back of a frame; the wire from which the picture will hang is tied to them.

Sight: The part of the picture that is visible from the front of the frame.

Slip liner: An inner frame, usually made of wood and placed between the art work and the outer frame or moulding. It is usually decorative, often covered in fabric and acts in much the same way as a mount.

Stretcher: A wooden frame to which the canvas, usually of an oil painting, is tautly tacked before it is framed.

Strut: An addition to the back of a frame that acts as a support and allows the frame to be free-standing.

Veneer: A thin layer of good quality wood laid over an inferior base. Veneers are often used to make decorative inlays.

Wash: A thin coating of diluted paint used to obtain a transparent or delicate finish.

Wash line: A wash applied in a band between inked or painted lines.

Wet mounting: A method of fixing a piece of artwork to a backing using a spray adhesive.

Window: The hole cut in the mount through which the artwork is visible.

INDEX